The Pope and the Freemasons

Also from Westphalia Press

westphaliapress.org

The Pope and the Freemasons

*The Letter "Humanum Genus" of the
Pope, Leo XIII, against Free-Masonry
and the Spirit of the Age*

WESTPHALIA PRESS
An imprint of the Policy Studies Organization

The Pope and the Freemasons
The Letter "Humanum Genus" of the Pope, Leo XIII,
against Free-Masonry and the Spirit of the Age

Westphalia Press
An imprint of Policy Studies Organization
dgutierrezs@ipsonet.org

For information:
Westphalia Press
1527 New Hampshire Ave., N.W.
Washington, D.C. 20036

ISBN-13: 978-1935907244
ISBN-10: 1935907247

Updated material and comments on this edition can be
found at the Westphalia Press website: westphaliapress.org

Note

In 1884, the celebrated indictment of Freemasonry by Pope Leo XIII elicited an equally celebrated reply by Albert Pike, the Grand Commander of the Scottish Rite of Freemasonry. This was hardly the first confrontation between the Roman Catholic Church and the Masons, but it proved to be a landmark.

Over the ensuing years, individual priests and bishops took a more tolerant attitude towards the membership in lodges by their parishioners, but despite goodwill on a local basis and claims that "Humanum Genus" had been supplanted, the official position of the Church has never changed.

So the encyclical and the response in 1884 have considerable importance. This reprints the original documents as the Grand Orient issued them.

DE SECTA MASSONUM.

SANCTISSIMI DOMINI NOSTRI LEONIS DIVINA PROVIDENTIA.

PAPAE XIII.

EPISTOLA ENCYCLICA AD PATRIARCHAS PRIMATES ARCHIEPISCOPOS ET EPISCOPOS CATHOLICI ORBIS VNIVERSOS GRATIAM ET COM-MVNIONEM CVM APOSTOLICA SEDE HABENTES.

VENERABILIBVS FRATRIBVS PATRIARCHIS PRIMATIBVS ARCHIEPIS-COPIS ET EPISCOPIS CATHOLICI ORBIS VNIVERSIS GRATIAM ET COMMVNIONEM CVM APOSTOLICA SEDE HABENTIBVS.

LEO PP. XIII.

VENERABILES FRATRES.
SALVTEM ET APOSTOLICAM BENEDICTIONEM.

HUMANUM GENUS, postea quam a creatore, munerumque cae-lestium largitore Deo, *invidia Diaboli*, miserrime defecit, in partes duas diversas adversasque discessit; quarum altera assidue pro veritate et virtute propugnat, altera pro iis, quae virtuti sunt veritatique contraria.—Alterum Dei est in terris regnum, vera scilicet Iesu Christi Ecclesia, cui qui volunt ex animo et convenienter ad salutem adhaerescere, necesse est Deo et Unigenito Filio eius tota mente ac summa voluntate servire; alterum Satanae est regnum, cuius in ditione et potestate sunt quicumque funesta ducis sui et primorum parentum exempla secuti, parere divinae aeternaeque legi recusant, et multa posthabito Deo, multa contra Deum contendunt. Duplex hoc regnum, duarum instar civitatum contrariis legibus contraria in studia abeuntium, acute vidit descriptique Augustinus, et utriusque efficientem caussam subtili brevitate complexus est, iis verbis: *fecerunt civitates duas amores duo: terrenam scilicet amor sui usque ad contemptum Dei; caelestem vero amor Dei usque ad contemptum sui.**—Vario ac multiplici cum armorum tum dimicationis genere altera adversus alteram omni saecu-lorum aetate conflixit, quamquam non eodem semper ardore atque impetu. Hoc autem tempore, qui deterioribus favent

**De Civit. Dei* Lib. xiv, c. 17.

partibus videntur simul conspirare vehementissimeque cuncti contendere, auctore et adiutrice ea, quam *Massonum* appellant, longe lateque diffusa et firmiter constituta hominum societate. Nihil enim iam dissimulantes consilia sua, excitant sese advesus Die numen audacissime, Ecclesiae sanctae perniciem palam aperteque moliuntur, idque eo proposito, ut gentes christianas partis per Iesum Christum Servatorem beneficiis, si fieri posset, funditus despolient.—Quibus Nos ingemiscentes malis, illud saepe ad Deum clamare, urgente animum caritate, compellimur: *Ecce inimici tui sonuerunt, et qui oderunt te, extulerunt caput. Super populum tuum malignaverunt consilium; et cogitaverunt adversus sanctos tuos, Dixerunt: venite et disperdamus eos de gente.**

In tam praesenti discrimine, in tam immani pertinacique christiani nominis oppugnatione, Nostrum est indicare periculum, de signare adversarios, horumque consiliis atque artibus, quantum possumus, resistere ut aeternum ne pereant quorum Nobis est commisa salus: et Iesu Christi regnum, quod tuendum accepimus, non modo stet et permaneat integrum, sed novis usque incrementis ubique terrarum amplificetur.

Romani Pontifices Decessores Nostri, pro salute populi christiani sedulo vigilantes, hunc tam capitalem hostem ex occultae coniurationis tenebris prosilientem, quis esset, quis vellet, celeriter agnoverunt; iidemque praecipientes cogitatione futur, principes simul et populos, signo velut dato, monuerunt ne se paratis ad decipiendum artibus insidiisque capi paterentur.—Prima significatio periculi per Clementem XII anno MDCCXXXVIII facta: cuius est a Benedicto XIV confirmata ac renovata Constitutio. Utriusque vestigiis ingressus est Pius VII: ac Leo XII Constitutione Apostolica *"Quo graviora"* superiorum Pontificum hac de re acta et decreta complexus, rata ac firma in perpetuum esse iussit. In eamdem sententiam Pius VIII, Gregorius XVI, persaepe vero Pius IX locuti sunt.

Videlicet cum sectae Massonicae institutum et ingenium compertum esset ex manifestis rerum indiciis, cognitione caussarum, prolatis in lucem legibus eius, ritibus, commentariis, ipsis saepe accedentibus testimoniis eorum qui essent conscii, haec Apostolica Sedes denuntiavit aperteque edixit, sectam Massonum, contra ius fasque constitutam, non minus esse christianae rei, quam civitati perniciosam; propositisque poenis quibus sotet Ecclesia gravius in sontes animadvertere, interdixit atque imperavit, ne quis illi nomen societati daret. Qua ex re irati gregales, earum vim sententiarum subterfugere aut debilitare se posse partim contemnendo, partim calumniando rati, Pontifices maximos, qui ea decreverant, criminati sunt aut non

*Ps. LXXXII, v. 2-4.

iusta decrevisse, aut modum in decernendo transisse. Hac same ratione Constitutionum Apostolicarum Clementis XII, Benedicti XIV, itemque Pii VII et Pii IX conati sunt auctoritatem et pondus eludere. Verum in ipsa illa societate non defuere, qui vel inviti faterentur, quod erat a romanis Pontificibus factum, id esse, spectara doctrina disciplinaque catholica, iure factum. In quo Pontificibus valde assentiri plures viri principes rerumque publicarum rectores visi sunt, quibus curae fuit societatem Massonicam vel apud Apostolicam Sedem arguere, vel per se, latis in id legibus, noxae damnare, ut in Hollandia, Austria, Helvetia, Hispania, Bavaria, Sabaudia, aliisque Italiae partibus.

Quod tamen prae ceteris, interest, prudentiam Decessorum Nostrorum rerum eventus comprobavit. Ipsorum enim providae paternaeque curae nec semper nec ubique optatos habuerunt exitus: idque vel hominum, qui in ea noxa essent, simultatione et astu, vel inconsiderata levitate ceterorum, quorum maxime interfuisset diligenter attendere. Quare unius saeculi dimidiatique spatio secta Massonum ad incrementa properavit opinione maiora; inferendoque sese per audaciam et dolos in omnes reipublicae ordines, tantum iam posse coepit, ut prope dominari in civitatibus videatur. Ex hoc tam celeri formidolosque cursu illa revera est in Ecclesiam, in potestatem principum, in salutem publicam pernicies consecuta, quam Decessores Nostri multo ante providerant. Eo enim perventum est, ut valde sit reliquo tempore metuendem non Ecclesiae quidem, quae longe firmius habet fundamentum, quam ut hominum operă labefactari queat, sed earum caussa civitatum, in quibus nimis polleat ea, de qua loquimur, aut aliae hominum sectae non absimiles, quae priori illi sese administras et satellites impertiunt.

His de caussis, ubi primum ad Ecclesiae gubernacula accessimus, vidimus planeque sensimus huic tanto malo resistere opposisu auctoritatis Nostrae, quoad fieri posset, oportere.—Sane opportunam saepius occasionem nacti, persecuti sumus praecipua quaedam doctrinarum capita, in quas Massonicarum opinionum influxisse maxime perversitas videbatur. Ita Litteris Nostris Encyclicis *"Quod Apostolic muneris"* aggressi sumus *Socialistarum* et *Communistarum* portenta convincere; aliis deinceps *"Arcanum"* veram germanamque notionem societatis domesticae, cuius est in matrimonio fons et origo, tuendum et explicandam curavimus: iis insuper, quarum intium est *"Diuturnum"* potestatis politicae formam ad principia christianae sapientiae expressam proposuimus, cum ipsa rerum natura, cum populorum principumque salute mirifice cohaerentem. Nunc autem, Decessorum Nostrorum exemplo, in Massonicam ipsam societatem, in doctrinam eius universam, et consilia, et sentiendi

consuetudinem et agendi, animum recta intendere decrevimus,
quo vis illius malefica magis magisque illustretur, idque valeat
ad funestae pestis prohibenda contagia.

Variae sunt hominum sectae, quae quamquam nomine, ritu,
forma origine differentes, cum tamen communione quadam
propositi summarumque sententiarum similitudine inter se con-
tineantur, re congruunt cum secta Massonum, quae cuiusdam
est instar centri unde abeunt et quo redeunt universae. Quae
quamvis nunc nolle admodum videantur latere in tenebris, et
suos agant coetus in luce oculisque civium, et suas edant
ephemeridas, nihilominus tamen, re pentius perspecta, penus
societatum clandestinarum moremque retinent. Plura quippe
in iis sunt arcanis similia, quae non externos solum, sed gregales
etiam bene multos exquisitissima diligentia celari lex est:
cuiusmodi sunt intima atque ultima consilia, summi factionum
principes, occulta quaedam et intestina conventicula: item
decreta, et qua via, quibus auxiliis perficienda. Huc sane facit
multiplex illud inter socios discrimen et iuris et officii et
muneris: huc rata ordinum graduumque distinctio, et illa, qua
reguntur, severitas disciplinae. Initiales spondere, immo
praecipuo sacramento iurare ut plurimum iubentur, nemini se
ullo unquam tempore ullove modo socios, notas, doctrinas indica-
turos. Sic ementita specie eodemque semper tenore simulationis
quam maxime Massones, ut olim Manichaei, laborant abdere
sese, nullosque, praeter, suos, habere testes. Latebras com-
modum quaerunt, sumpta sibi litteratorum sophorumve persona,
eruditionis caussa sociatorum; habent in lingua promptum
cultioris urbanitatis studium, tenuioris plebis caritatem: unice
velle se meliores res multitudini quaerere, et quae habentur in
civili societate commoda cum quamplurimis communicare. Quae
quidem consilia quamvis vera essent, nequaquam tamen in istis
omnia. Praetere qui cooptati sunt, promittant ac recipiant
necesse est, ducibus ac magistris se dicto audientes futuros cum
obsequio fideque maxima: ad quemlibet eorum nutum significa-
tionemque paratos, imperata facturos: si secus fecerint, tum
dira omnia ac mortem ipsam non recusare. Revera si qui
prodidisse disciplinam vel mandatis restitisse iudicentur, sup-
plicium de iis non raro sumitur, et audacia quidem ac dexteri-
tate tanta, ut speculatricem ac vindicem 'scelerum iustitiam
sicarius persaepe fallat.—Atqui simulare, et velle in occulto
latere: obligare sibi homines, tanquam mancipia, tenacissimo
nexu, nec satis declarata caussa: alieno addictos arbitrio ad
omne facinus adhibere: armare ad caedem dextras, quaesita
impunitate peccandi, immanitas quaedum est, quam rerum
natura non partitur. Quapropter societatem, de qua loquimur,
cum iustitia et naturali honestate pugnare, ratio et veritas ipsa
convincit.

Eo vel magis, quod ipsius naturam ab honestate dissidentem alia quoque argumenta eademque illustria redarguunt. Ut enim magna sit in hominibus astutia celandi consuetudoque mentiendi, fieri tamen non potest, ut unaquaeque caussa ex iis rebus, quarum caussa est, qualis in se sit non aliqua ratione appareat. *Non potest arbor bona malos fructus facere; neque arbor mala bonus fructus facere.** Fructus autem secta Massonum perniciosos gignit maximaque acerbitate permixtos. Nam ex certissimis indiciis, quae supra commemoravimus, erumpit illud, quod est consiliorum suorum ultimum, scilicet evertere funditus omnem eam, quam instituta christiana pepererunt, disciplinam religionis reique publicae, novam que ad ingenium suum extruere, ductis e medio *Naturalismo* fundamentis et legibus.

Haec, quae diximus aut dicturi sumus, de secta Massonica intelligi opertet spectata in genere suo, et quatenus sibı cognatas foederatesque complectitur societates: non autem de sectatoribus earum singulis. In quorum numero utique possunt esse, nec pauci, qui quamvis culpa non careant quod sese istius modi implicuerint societatibus, tamen nec sint flagitiose factorum per se ipsi participes, et illud ultimum ignorent quod illae nituntur adipisci. Similiter ex consociationibus ipsis nonnullae fortasse nequaquam probant conclusiones quasdam extremas, quas, cum ex principiis communibus necessario consequantur, consentaneum esset amplexari, nisi per se foeditate sua turpitudo ipsa deterreret. Item nonnullas locorum temporumve ratio suadet minora conari, quam aut ipsas vellent aut ceterae solent; non idcirco tamen alienae a Massonico foedere putandae, quia Massonicum foedus non tam est ab actis perfectisque rebus, quam a sententiarum summa iudicandum.

Iamvero Naturalistarum caput est, quod nomine ipso satis declarant, humanam naturam humanamque rationem cunctis in rebus magistram esse et principem oportere. Quo constituto, officia erga Deum vel minus curant, vel opinionibus pervertunt errantibus et vagis. Negant enim quicquam esse Deo auctore traditum: nullum probant de religione dogma, nihil veri, quod non hominum intelligentia comprehendat, nullum magistrum, cui propter auctoritatem officii sit iure credendum. Qouniam autem munus est Ecclesiae catholicea singulare sibique unice proprium doctrinas, divinitus acceptas auctoritatemque magesterii cum ceteris ad salutem caelestibus adiumentis plene complecti et incorrupta integritate tueri, idcirco in ipsam maxima est inimicorum iracundia impetusque conversus.—Nunc vero in iis rebus, quae religionem attingunt, spectetur quid agat, praesertim ubi est ad agendi licentiam liberior, secta Massonum; omninoque iudicetur, nonne plane re exequi Naturalistarum

*Matt. VII, 18.

decreta velle videatur. Longo sane pertinacique labore in id datur opera, nihil ut Ecclesiae magisterium nihil auctoritas in civitate possit: ob eamque caussam vulgo praedicant et pugnant, rem sacram remque civilem esse penitus distrahendas. Quo facto saluberrimam religionis catholicae virtutem a legibus, ab administratione reipublicae excludunt: illudque est consequens, ut praeter instituta aut praecepta Ecclesiae totas constituendas putent civitates. Nec vero non curare Ecclesiam, optimam ducem setis habent, non hostiliter faciendo laeserint. Et sane fundamenta ipsa religionis catholicae adoriri fando, scribendo, docendo, impune licet: non iuribus Ecclesiae parcitur non munera, quibus est divinitus aucta, salva sunt. Agendarum rerum facultas quam minima illi relinquitur, idque legibus specie quidem non nimis vim inferentibus, re vera natis aptis ad impediendam libertatem. Item impositas Clero videmus leges singulares et graves, multum ut ei de numero, multum de rebus necessariis in dies decedat: reliquias bonorum Ecclesiae maximis adstrictas vinculis, potestati et arbitrio administratorum reipublicae permissas: sodalitates ordinum religiosorum sublatas, dissipatas.—At vero in Sedem Apostolicam romanumque Pontificem longe est inimicorum incitata contentio. Is quidem primum fictis de caussis deturbatus est propugnaculo libertatis iurisque sui, principatu civili: mox in statum compulsus iniquum simul et obiectis undique difficultatibus intolerabilem: donec ad haec tempora perventum est, quibus sectarum fautores, quod abscondite secum agitarant diu, aperte denunciant, sacram tollendam Pontificum potestatem, ipsumque divino iure institutum funditus delendum Pontificatum. Quam rem, si cetera deessent, satis indicat hominum qui conscii sunt testimonium, quorum plerique cum saepe alias, tum recenti memoria rursus hoc Massonum verum esse declararunt, velle eos maxime exercere catholicum nomen implacabilibus inimicitiis, nec ante quieturos, quam excisa omnia viderint, quaecumque summi Pontifices religionis caussa instituissent.—Quod si, qui adscribuntur in numerum, nequaquam eiurare conceptis verbis instituta catholica iubentur, id sane tantum abest, ut consiliis Massonum repugnet, ut potius adserviat. Primum enim simplices et incautos facile decipiunt hac via, multoque pluribus invitamenta praebent. Tum vera obviis quibuslibet ex quovis religionis ritu accipiendis, hoc assequuntur, ut re ipsa suadeant magnum illum huius temporis errorem, religionis curam relinqui oportere in mediis, nec ullum esse inter genera discrimen. Quae quidem ratio comparata ad interitum est religionum omnium, nominatim ad catholicae, quae cum una ex omnibus vera sit, exaequari cum ceteris sine iniuria summa non potest.

Sed longius Naturalistae progrediuntur. In maximis enim rebus tota errare via audacter ingressi, praecipiti cursu ad extrema delabuntur, sive humanae imbecilitate naturae, sive consilio iustas superbiae poenas repetenis Dei. Ita fit, ut illis ne ea quidem certa et fixa permaneant, quae naturali lumine rationis perspiciuntur, qualia profecto illa sunt, Deum esse, animos hominum ab omni esse materiae concretione segregatos, eosdemque immortales.—Atqui secta Massonum ad hos ipsos scopulos non dissimili cursus errore adhaerescit. Quamvis enim Deum esse generatim profiteantur, id tamen non haerere in singulorum mentibus firma assensione iudicioque stabli constitutum, ipsi sibi sunt testes. Neque enim dissimulant, hanc de Deo quaestionem maximum apud ipsos esse fontem caussamque dissidii: immo non mediocrem hac ipsa de re constat extitisse inter eos proximo etiam tempore contentionem. Re autem vera initiatis magnam secta licentiam dat, ut alterutrum liceat suo iure defendere, Deum esse, Deum nullum esse: et qui nullum esse praefracte contendant, tam facile initiantur, quam qui Deum esse opinantur quidem, sed de eo prava sentiunt, ut Pantheistae solent: quod nihil est aliud, quam divinae naturae absurdum quamdam speciem retinere, veritatem tollere. Quo everso infirmatove maximo fundamento, consequens est ut illa quoque vacillent, quae natura admonente cognoscuntur, cunctas res libera creatoris Dei voluntate extitisse: mundum providentia regi: nullum esse animorum interitum: huic, quae in terris agitur, hominum vitae successuram alteram eamque sempiternam.

His autem dilapsis, quae sunt tamquam naturae principia, ad cognitionem usumque praecipua, quales futuri sint privati publicique mores, facile apparet.—Silemus de virtutibus divinioribus, quas absque singulari Dei munere et dono nec execere potest quisquam, nec consequi: quarem profecto necesse est nullum in iis vestigium reperiri, qui redemptionem generis humani, qui gratiam caelestem, qui sacramenta, adipiscendamque in caelis felicitatem pro ignotis aspernantur.—Do officiis loquimur, quae a naturali honestate ducuntur. Mundi enim opifex idemque providus gubernator Deus: lex aeterna naturalem ordine conservari iubens, perturbari vetans: ultimus hominum finis multo excelsior rebus humanis extra haec mundana hospitia constitutus: hi fontes, haec principia sunt totius iustitia et honestatis. Ea si tollantur, quod Naturalistae idemque Massones solent, continuo iusti et iniusti scientia ubi consistat, et quo se tueatur omnino non habebit. Et sane disciplina morum, quae Massonum familiae probatur unice, et qua informari adolescentem aetatem contendunt oportere, ea est quam et *civicam* nominant et *solutam ac liberam;* scilicet in qua opinio nulla sit religionis inclusa. At vero quam inops illa sit, quam firmitatis expers, et ad omnem auram cupiditatum mobilis, satis ostenditur ex iis, qui partim iam apparent, poenitendis fructibus. Ubi enim regnare illa liberius coepit, demota loco institutione christiana, ibi celeriter deperire probi integrique mores: opinionum tetra portenta convalescere: plenoque gradu audacia ascendere maleficiorum. Quod quidem vulgo conqueruntur et deplorant: idemque non pauci ex iis, qui minime vellent, perspicua veritate compulsi, haud raro testantur.

Praeterea, quoniam, est hominum natura prima labe peccati inquinata, et ob hanc caussam multo ad vitia quam ad virtutes propensior, hoc omnino ad honestatem requiritur, cohibere motus animi turbidos et appetitus obedientes facere rationi. In quo certamine despicientia saepissime abhibenda est rerum humanarum, maximque exhauriendi labores ac molestiae, quo suum semper teneat ratio victrix principatum. Verum Naturalistae et Massones, nulla adhibita iis rebus fide, quas Deo auctore cognovimus, parentem generis humani negant deliquisse: proptereaque liberum arbitrium nihil *viribus attenuatum et inclinatum* putant. Quin immo exaggerantes naturae virtutem et excellentiam, in eaque principium et norman iustitiae unice collocantes, ne cogitare quidem possunt, ad sedandos illius impetus regendosque appetitus assidua contentione et summa opus esse constantia. Ex quo videmus vulgo suppeditari hominibus illecebras multas cupiditatum: ephemeridas commentariosque nulla nec temperantia nec verecundia: ludos scenicos ad licentiam insignes: argumenta artium ex iis, quas vocant *verismi*, legibus proterve quaesita: excogitata subtiliter vitate artificia delicatae et molis: omnia denique conquisita voluptatum blandimenta, quibus sopita virtus conniveat. In quo flagitiose faciunt, sed sibi admodum constant qui expectationem tollunt bonorum caelestium, omnemque ad res mortales felicitatem abiiciunt et quasi demergunt in terram.—Quae autem commemorata sunt illud confirmare potest non tam re, quam dictu inopinatum. Cum enim hominibus versutis et callidis nemo fere soleat tam obnoxie servire, quam quorum est cupiditatum dominatu enervatus et fractus animus, reperti in secta Massonum sunt, qui edicerent ac proponerent, consilio et arte enitendum ut infinita vitiorum licentia exsaturetur multitudo: hoc enim facto, in potestate sibi et arbitrio ad quaelibet audenda facile futuram.

Quod ad convictum attinet domesticum, his fere continetur omnis Naturalistarum disciplina. Matrimonium ad negotiorum contrahendorum petinere genus: rescindi ad voluntatem eorum, qui contraxerint, iure posse; penes gubernatores rei civilis esse in maritale vinclum potestatem. In educandis liberis nihil de religione praecipiatur ex certa destinataque sententia: integrum singulis esto, cum adoleverit aetas, quod maluerint sequi.—Atqui haec ipsa assentiuntur plane Massones: neque assentiuntur solum, sed iamdiu student in morem consuetudinemque deducere. Multis iam in regionibus, iisdemque catholici nominis, constitutum est ut, praeter coniunctas ritu civili, iustae ne habeantur nuptiae:

alibi divortia fieri, lege licet: alibi, ut quamprimum liceat, datur opera. Ita ad illud festinat cursus, ut matrimonia in aliam naturam convertantur, hoc est in coniunctiones instabiles et fluxas, quas libido conglutinet, et eadem mutata dissolvat.—Summa autem conspiratione voluntatum illuc etiam spectat secta Massonum, ut institutionem ad se rapiat adolescentium. Mollem enim et flexibilem aetatem facile se posse sentiunt arbitratu suo fingere, et, quo velint, torquere: eaque re nihil esse opportunis ad sobolem civium, qualem ipsi meditantur, talem reipublicae educendam. Quocirca in educatione doctrinaque puerili nullas Ecclesiae ministrii nec magisterri nec vigilantiae sinunt esse partes: pluribusque iam locis consecuti sunt, ut omnis sit penes viros laicos adolescentium institutio: itemque ut in mores informandos nihil admisceatur de iis quae hominem iungent Deo, permagnis sanctissimisque officiis.

Sequuntur civilis decreta prudentiae. Quo in genera statuunt Naturalistae, homines eodoem esse iure omnes, et aequa ac pari in omnes partes conditione: unumquemque esse natura liberum: imperandi alteri ius habere neminem: velle autem, ut homines cuiusquam auctoritati pareant, aliunde quam ex ipsis quaesitae, id quidem esse vim inferre. Omnia igitur in libero populo esse: imperium iussu vel concessu populi teneri, ita quidem, ut, mutata voluntate populari, principes de gradu deiici vel invitos liceat. Fontem omnium iurium officiorumque civilium vel in multitudine inesse, vel in potestate gubernante civitatem, eaque novissimis informata disciplinis. Praeterea atheam esse rempublicam oportere: in variis religionis formis nullam esse caussam, cur alia alii anteponatur: eodem omnes loco habendas.

Haec autem ipsa Massonibus aeque placere, et ad hanc similitudinem atque exemplar velle eos constituere res publicas, plus est cognitum, quam ut demonstrari oporteat. Iamdiu quippe omnibus viribus atque opibus id aperte moliuntur: et hoc ipso expediunt viam audacioribus non paucis ad peiora praecipitantibus, ut qui aequationem cogitant communionemque omnium bonorum, deleto ordinum et fortunarum in civitatem descrimine.

Secta igitur Massonum quid sit, et quod iter affectet ex his quae summatim attigimus, satis elucet. Praecipua ipsorum dogmata tam valde a ratione ac tam a manifesto discrepant, ut nihil possit esse perversius. Religionem et Ecclesiam, quam Deus ipse condidit, idemque ad immortalitatem tuetur, velle demoliri, moresque et instituta ethnicorum duodeviginti saeculorum intervallo revocare, insignis stultitiae est impietatisque audacissimae. Neque illud vel horribile minus, vel levius ferendum, quod beneficia repudientur per Iesum Christum benigne parta neque hominibus solum singulis, sed vel familia vel communitate civili consociatis: quae beneficia ipso habentur inimicorum iudicio testimonique maxima. In huiusmodi voluntate vesana et tetra recognosci propemodum videtur posse illud ipsum, quo Satanas in Iesum Christum ardet inexpiabile odium ulciscendique libido.—Similiter illud alterum, quod Massones vehementer conantur, recti atque honesti praecipua fundamenta evertere, adiutoresque se praebere iis, qui more pecudum quodcumque libeat, idem licere vellent, nihil est aliud quam genus humanum cum ignominia et dedecore ad interitum impellere.—Augent vero malum ea, quae in societatem cum domesticam tum civilem intenduntur pericula. Quod enim alias exposuimus, inest in matrimonio sacrum et religiosum quiddam omnium fere et gentium et aetatum consensu: divina autem lege cautum esse, ne coniugia dirimi liceat. Ea si profana fiant, si distrahi liceat, consequatur in familia ncesse est turba et confusio, excidentibus de dignitate feminis incerta rerum suarum incolumitatisque sobole.—Curam vero de religione publice adhibere nullam, et in rebus civicis ordinandis, gerendis, Deum nihilo magis respicere, quam si omnino non esset, temeritas est ipsis ethnicis inaudita; quorum in animo sensuque erat sic penitus affixa non solum opinio Deorum, sed religionis publicae necessitas ut inveniri urbem facilius sine solo, quam sine Deo posse arbitrarentur. Revera humani generis societas, ad quam sumus natura facti, a Deo constituta est naturae parente; ab eoque tamquam a principo et fonte tota vis et perennitas manat innumerabilium, quibus illa abundat, bonorum. Igitur quemadmodum singuli pie Deum sancteque colere ipso naturae voce admonemur, propterea quod vitam et bona quae comitantur vitae a Deo accepimus, sic eamdem ob causam populi et civitates. Idcirco qui solutam omni religionis officio civilem communitatem volunt, perspicuum est non iniuste solum, sed etiam indocte absurdeque facere.—Quod vero homines ad coniunctionem congregationemque civilem Dei voluntate nascuntur, et potestas imperandi vinculum est civilis societatis tam necessarium ut, eo sublato, illam repente disrumpi necesse sit, consequens est ut imperandi auctoritatem idem gignat, qui genuit societatem. Ex quo intelligitur, imperium in quo sit, quicumque is est, ministrum esse Dei. Quapropter, quatenus finis et natura societatus humanae postulant, legitimae potestati iusta praecipienti aequum est parere perinde ac numini omnia moderantis Dei: illudque in primis a veritate abhorret, in populi esse voluntate positum obedientiam, cum libitum fuerit, abiicere.—Similiter pares inter se homines esse universos, nemo dubitat, si genus et natura communis, si finis ultimus unicuique ad assequendum propositus, si ea, quae inde sponte fluunt, iura et officia spectentur. At vero quia ingenia omnium paria esse non possunt, et alius ab alio distat vel animi vel corporis viribus, plurimaeque sunt morum, voluntatis, naturarum dissimilitudines, idcirco nihil tam est repugnans retioni, quam una velle comprehensione omnia complecti, et illam omnibus partibus expletam aequabilitatem ad vitae civilis insti-

tuta traducere. Quemadmodum perfectus corporis habitus ex-
diversorum existit iunctura et compositione membrorum, quae
forma usuque different compacta tamen et suis distributa locis
complexionem efficiunt pulcram specie, firman viribus, utilitate
necessari: ita in republica hominum quasi partium infinita propemodum est dissimilitudo: qui si habeantur pares arbitriumque
singuli suum sequantur, species erit civitatis nulla deformoir: si
vero dignitatis, studiorum, artium, distinctis gradibus, apte ad
commune bonum conspirent, bene constitutae civitatas imaginem
referent congruentemque naturae.

Certerum ex iis, quos commemoraviums, turbulentis erroribus,
maximae sunt civitatibus extimescendae formidines. Nam sublato Dei metu legumque divarum verecundia, despecta principum
auctoritate, permissa probataque seditionum libidine, proiectis
ad licentiam cupiditatibus popularibus, nullo nisi poenarum
freno, necessario secutara est rerum omnium commutatio et
eversio. Hanc immo commutationem eversionemque consulto
meditantur, ibque prae se ferunt, plurimi **Communistarum** et
Socialistarum consociati greges: quorum coeptis alienam ne se
dixerit secta Massonum, quae et consiliis eorum admodum favet,
et summa sententiarum capita cum ipsis habet communia. Quod
si nec continuo nec ubique ad extrema experiendo decurrunt,
non ipsorum est disciplinae, non voluntati tribuendum, sed virtuti religionis divinae, quae extingui non potest, itemque saniori
hominum parti, qui societatum clandestinarum recusantes servi-
tutem, insanos earum conatus forti animo refutant.

Atque utinam omnes stirpem ex fructibus iudicarent, et malo-
rum quae premunt, periculorum quae impendent, semen et initium
agnoscerent! Res est cum hoste fallaci et doloso, qui serviens
auribus populorum et principum, utrosque mollibus sententiis et
assentatione cepit. Insinuando sese ad viros principes simulatione
amicitiae, hoc spectarunt Massones, illos ipsos habere ad oppri-
mendum catholicum nomen socios et adiutores potentes: quibus
quo maiores admoverent stimulos, pervicaci calumnia Ecclesiam
criminati sunt de potestate iuribusque regiis cum principibus in-
vidiose contendere. His interim artibus quaesita securitate et
audacia, plurimum pollere in regendis civitatibus coerperunt, ce-
terum parati imperiorum fundamenta quartere, et insequi principes civitatis, insimulare eiicere, quoties facere secus in guber-
nando viderentur, quam illi maluissent. Haud absimili modo
populos assentando ludificati sunt. Libertatem prosperitatemque
publicam pleno ore personantes, et per Ecclesiam Principesque
summos stetisse, quominus ex iniqua servitute et egestate multitudo eriperetur, populo imposuerrunt, eumque rerum novarum
sollicitatum siti in oppugnationem utriusque potestatis incita-
verunt. Nihilominus tamen speratarum commoditatum maior
est expectatio, quam veritas: immo vero peius oppressa plebes

magnam partem iis ipsis carere cogitur miseriarum solatiis, quae, compositis ad christiana instituta rebus, facile **et** abunde reperire potuisset. Sed quotquot contra ordinem nituntur divina providentia constitutum, has dare solent superbiae poenas, ut ibi afflictam et miseram offendant fortunam, unde prosperam et ad vota fluentem temere expectavissent.

Ecclesia vero, quod homines obedire praecipue et maxime iubet summo omnium principi Deo, iniuria et falso putaretur aut civili invidere potestati, aut sibi quicquam de iure principum arrogare. Immo quod civili potestati aequum est reddere, id plane indicio conscientiaque officii decernit esse reddendum. Quod vero ab ipso Deo ius arcessit imperandi, magna est ad civilem auctoritatem dignitatis accessio, et observantiae benevolentiaeque civium colligendae adiumentum non exiguum. Eadam amica pacis, altrix concordiae, materna omnes caritate complecitur; et iuvandis mortalibus unice intenta, iustitiam opertere docet cum clementia, imperium cum acquitate, leges cum moderatione coniungere; nullius ius violandum, ordini tranquillitatique publicae serviendum, inopiam miseroum, quam maxime fieri potest, privatim et publice sublevendam. *Sed propterea putant*, ut verba usurpemus Augustini, *vel putari volunt, christianam doctrionam ulitati non convenire reipublicae, quia nolunt stare rempublicam firmitate virtutum, sed impunitate vitorum.** Quibis cognitis hoc esset civili prudentiae admodum congruens, et incolumitati communi necessarium, principes et populos non cum Massonibus ad labefactandam Ecclesiam, sed cum Ecclesia ad frangendos Massonum impetus conspirare.

Utcumque erit, in hoc tam gravi ac nimis iam pervagato malo Nostrarum est partium, Venerabiles Fratres, applicare animum ad quaerenda remedia. Quia vero spem remedii optiman et fir· missimam intelligimus esse in virtute sitam religionis divinae, quam tanto peius Massones oderunt, quanto magis pertimescunt, ideo caput esse censemus saluberrimam istam adversus communem hostem advocatam adhibere virtutem. Itaque quaecumque romani Pontifices Decessores Nostri decreverunt inceptis et conatibus sectae Massonum impediendis: quaecumque aut deterrendi ab eiusmodi societatibus aut revocandi caussa sanxerunt, omnia Nos et singula rata habemus atque auctoritate Nostra Apostolica confirmamus. In quo quidem plurimum voluntate christianorum confisi, per salutem singulos suam precamur quaesumusque, ut religioni habeant vel minimum ab iis discedere, quae hac de re Sedes Apostolica praeceperit.

Vos autem, Venerabiles Fratres, rogamus, flagitamus, ut collata Nobiscum opera, extirpate impuram hanc lucem quae serpit per omnes reipublicae venas, enixe studeatis. Tuenda Vobis est

---

**Epist.* CXXXVII, al. III, ad Volusianum, c. v. n. 20.

gloria Dei, salus proximorum: quibus rebus in dimicando propos
situs, non animus Vos, non fortitudo deficiet. Erit prudentiae
vestrae iudicare, quibus potissimum rationibus ea, quae obstabunt
et impedient, eluctanda videantur. Sed quoniam pro auctoritate
officii Nostri par est probabilem aliquam rei gerendae rationem
Nosmetipsos demonstrare, sic statuite, primum omnium redden-
dam Massonibus esse suam, dempta persona, faciem: populosque
sermone et datis etiam in id Litteris episcopalibus edocendos, quae
sint societatum eius generis in blandiendo alliciendoque artificia,
et in opinionibus pravitas, et in actionibus tupitudo. Quod plu-
ries Decessores Nostri confirmarunt, nomen sectae Massonum
dare nemo sibi quapiam de caussa licere putet, si catholica pro-
fessio et salus sua tanti apud eum sit, quanti esse debet. Ne
quem honestas assimulata decipiat: potest enim quibusdam videri,
nihil postulare Massones, quod aperte sit religionis morumve
sanctitati contrarium: veruntamen quia sectae ipsius tota in vitio
flagitioque est et ratio et caussa, congregare se cum eis, eosve
quoquo modo iuvare, rectum est non licere.

Deinde assiduitate dicendi hortandisque pertrahere multitudi-
nem opertet ad praecepta religionis diligenter addiscenda: cuius
rei gratia valde suademus, ut scriptis et concionibus tempestivis
elementa rerum sanctissimarum explanentur, quibus christiana
philosophia continetur. Quod illuc pertinent ut mentes hominum
eruditione sanentur et contra moltiplices errorum formas et varia
invitamenta vitiorum muniantur in hac praesertim et scribendi
licentia et inexhausta aviditate discendi. Magnum sane opus:
in quo tamen particeps et socius laborum vestrorum praecipue fu-
turus est Clerus, si fuerit, Vobis adnitentibus, a disciplina vitae,
a scientia litterarum probe instructus. Verum tam honesta
caussa tamque gravis advocatam desiderat industriam virorum
laicorum, qui religionis et patriae caritatem cum probitate doctrinaque coniungant. Consociatia utriusque ordinis viribus, date
operam, Venerabiles Fratres, ut Ecclesiam penitus et cognoscant
homines et caram habeant; eius enim quanto cognitio fuerit
amorque maior, tanto futurum maius est societatem clandestinarum fastidium et fuga. Quocirca non sine causta idoneam hanc
occasionem nacti, renovamus illud quod alias exposuimus, Ordinem Tertium Franciscalium, cuius paullo ante temperavimus
prudenti lenitate disciplinam, perquam studiose propagare tue-
rique oportere. Eius enim, ut est ab auctore suo constitutus,
haec tota est ratio, vocare homines ad imitationem Iesu Christi,
ad amorem Ecclesiae, ad omnia virtutum christianarum officia:
propteraque multum posse debet ad societatum nequissimarum
supprimendam contagionem. Novetur itaque quotidianis incrementis isthaec sancta sodalitas, unde cum multi expectari possunt
fructus, tum ille egregius, ut traducantur animi ad libertatem,
ad fraternitatem, ad aequalitatem iuris: non qualia Massones ab-

surde cogitant, sed qualia et Iesus Christus humano generi comparavit et Franciscus secutus est. Libertatem dicimus *filiorum Dei*, per quam nec Satanae, nec cupiditatibus, improbissimis dominis serviamus: fraternitatem, cuius in Deo communi omnium procreatore et parente consistat origo: aequalitatem, quae iustitiae caritatisque constituta fundamentis, non omnia tollat inter homines discrimina, sed ex vitae, officiorum, studiorumque varietate mirum illum consensum efficiat et quasi concentum, qui natura ad utilitatem pertinet dignitatemque civilem.

Tertio loco una quaedam res est, a maioribus sapienter instituta, eademque temporum cursu intermissa, quae tamquam exemplar et forma ad simile aliquid valere in praesentia potest.— Scholas seu collegia opificum intelligimus, rebus simul et moribus, duce religione, tutandis. Quorum collegiorum utilitatem si maiores nostri diuturni temporis usu et periclitatione senserunt, sentiet fortasse magis aetas nostra, propterea quod singularem habent ad elidendas sectarum vires opportunitatem. Qui mercede manuum inopiam tolerant, praeterquam quod ipsa eorum conditione uni ex omnibus sunt caritate solatioque dignissimi, maxime praetereo patent illecebris grassantium per fraudes et dolos. Quare iuvandi sunt maiore qua potest benignitate, et invitandi ad societates honestas, ne pertrahantur ad turpes. Huius rei caussa collegia illa magnopere vellemus auspiciis patrocinioque Episcoporum convenienter temporibus ad salutem plebis passim restituta. Nec mediocriter Nos delectat, quod pluribus iam locis sodalitates eiusmodi, itemque coetus patronorum constituti sint: quibus propositum utrisque est honestam proletariorum classem iuvare, eorum liberos, familias, praesidio et custodia tegere, in eisque pietatis studia, religionis doctrinam, cum integritate morum tueri.—In quo genere silere hoc loco nolumus illam spectaculo exemploque insignem, de populo inferioris ordinis tam praeclare meritam societatem, quae a Vincentio patre nominatur. Cognitum est quid agat, quid velit: scilicet tota in hoc est, ut egentibus et calamitosis suppetias eat ultro, idque sagacitate modestiaque mirabili: quae quo minus videri vult, eo est ad caritatem christianam melior, ad miseriarum levamen opportunior.

Quarto loco, quo facilius id quod volumus assequamur, fidei vigiliaeque vestrae maiorem in modum commendamus iuventutem, ut quae spes est societatis humanae.—Partem curarum vestrarum in eius institutione maximam ponite: nec providentiam putetis ullam fore tantam, quin sit adhibenda maior, ut iis adolescens aetas prohibeatur et scholis et magistris un de pestilens sectarum afflatus metuatur. Parentes, magistri pietatis, Curiones inter christianae doctrinae praeceptiones insistant, Vobis auctoribus opportune commonere liberos et alumnos de eiusmodi societatum flagitiosa natura, et ut mature cavere discant artes fraudulentas et varias, quas earum propagatores usurpare ad illaqueandos homines consueverunt. Immo qui adolescentulos ad sacra percipienda rite erudiunt, non inepte fecerint, si adducant singulos ut statuant ac recipitant, inscientibus parentibus, aut non auctore vel Curione vel conscientiae iudice, nulla se unquam societate obligaturos.

Verum probe intelligimus communes labores nostros evellendis his agro Dominico perniciosis seminibus haudquaquam pares futuros, nisi caelestis dominus vineae ad id quod intendimus benigne adiuverit.—Igitur eis opem auxiliumque implorare necesse est studio vehementi ac sollicito, quale et quantum vis periculi et magnitudo necessitatis requirunt. Effert se insolenter, successu gestiens, secta Massonum, nec ullum iam videtur pertinaciae factura modum. Asseclae eius universi nefario quodam foedere et occulta consiliorum communitate iuncti operam sibi mutuam tribuunt, et alteri alteros ad rerum malarum excitant audaciam. Oppugnatio tam vehemens propugnationem postulat parem: nimirum boni omnes amplissimam quamdam coeant opus est et agendi societatem et precandi. Ab eis itaque petimus, ut concordibus animis contra progredientem sectarum vim conferti immotique consistant: iidemque multum gementes tendant Deo manus supplices, ab eoque contendant, ut christianum floreat vigeatque nomen: necessari libertate Ecclesia potiatur: redeant ad sanitatem devii: errores veritati, vitia virtuti aliquando concedant.—Adiutricem et interpretem adhibeamus Mariam Virginem matrem Die, ut quae a conceptu ipso Satanam vicit, eadem se impertiat improbarum sectarum potentem, in quibus perspicuum est contumaces illos mali daemonis spiritus cum indomita perfidia et simulatione reviviscere.—Obtestemur principem Angelorum caelestium, depulsorem hostium infernorum, Michaelem; item Iosephvm Virginis sanctissimae sponsum, Ecclesiae catholicae patronum caelestem salutarem; Petrvm et Pavllvm Apostolos magnos, fidei christiane satores et vindices invictos. Horum patrocinio et communium perseverantia precum futurum confidimus ut coniecto in tot discrimina hominum generi opportune Deus benigneque succurrat.

Caelestium vero munerum et benevolentiae Nostrae testem Vobis, Venerabiles Fratres, Clero populoque universo vigilantiae vestra commisso Apostolicam Benedictionem peramanter in Domino impertimus.

Datum Romae apud S. Petrum die XX Aprilis An. MDCCCLXXXIV, Pontificatus Nostri Anno Septimo.

LEO PP. XIII.

THE MASONIC SECT.

LEO, POPE, XIII.

To all venerable Patriarchs, Primates, Archbishops, and Bishops in the Catholic world who have grace and communion with the Apostolic See:

VENERABLE BROTHERS:

Health and the Apostolic Benediction!

THE HUMAN RACE, after, by the malice of the devil, it had departed from God, the Creator and Giver of heavenly gifts, divided itself into two different and opposing parties, one of which assiduously combats for truth and virtue, the other for those things which are opposed to virtue and to truth. The one is the Kingdom of God on earth—that is, the Church of Jesus Christ; those who desire to adhere to which from their soul and conducively to salvation must serve God and His only begotten Son with their whole mind and their whole will. The other is the kingdom of Satan, in whose dominion and power are all who have followed his sad example and that of our first parents. They refuse to obey divine and eternal law, and strive for many things to the neglect of God and for many against God. This twofold kingdom, like two states with contrary laws working in contrary directions, Augustine clearly saw and described, and comprehended the efficient cause of both with subtle brevity in these words: "Two loves have made two states: the love of self to the contempt of God has made the earthly, but the love of God to the contempt of self has made the heavenly." (De Civ. Dei, lib. xiv., chap. 17.)

The one fights the other with different kinds of weapons, and battles at all times, though not always with the same ardor and fury. In our days, however, those who follow the evil one seem to conspire and strive all together under the guidance and with the help of that society of men spread all over, and solidly established, which they call Freemasons. Not dissimulating their intentions, they vie in attacking the power of God; they openly and ostensibly strive to damage the Church, with the

purpose to deprive thoroughly if possible Christian people of
the benefits brought by the Saviour Jesus Christ.

Seeing these evils, we are compelled by charity in our soul to
say often to God: "For lo! Thy enemies have made noise; and
they that hate Thee have lifted up the head. They have taken
malicious counsel against Thy people, and have consulted
against Thy saints. They have said: Come and let us destroy
them, so that they be not a nation." (Ps. lxxxii., 2-4.)

In such an impending crisis, in such a great and obstinate
warfare upon Christianity, it is our duty to point out the
danger, exhibit the adversaries, resist as much as we can their
schemes and tricks, lest those whose salvation is in our hands
should perish eternally: and that the kingdom of Jesus Christ,
which we have received in trust, not only may stay and remain
intact, but may continue to increase all over the world by new
additions.

The Roman Pontiffs, our predecessors, watching constantly
over the safety of the Christian people, early recognized this
capital enemy rushing forth out of the darkness of hidden conspiracy, and, anticipating the future in their mind, gave the
alarm to princes and people, that they should not be caught by
deceptions and frauds.

Clement XII. first signalized the danger in 1738, and Benedict XIV. renewed and continued his Constitution. Pius VII.
followed them both; and Leo XII., by the Apostolic Constitution
—quo graviora—recapitulating the acts and decrees of the
above Pontiffs about the matter, validated and confirmed them
forever. In the same way spoke Pius VIII., Gregory XVI., and
very often Pius IX.

The purpose and aim of the Masonic sect having been discovered from plain evidence, from the cognition of causes, its
laws, Rites and commentaries having come to light and been
made known by the additional depositions of the associated
members, this Apostolic See denounced and openly declared that
the sect of Masons is established against law and honesty, and
is equally a danger to Christianity as well as to society; and,
threatening those heavy punishments which the Church uses
against the guilty ones, she forbade the society, and ordered
that none should give his name to it. Therefore the angry
Masons, thinking that they would escape the sentence or partially destroy it by despising or calumniating, accused the Pope
who made those decrees of not having made a right decrcee or
of having overstepped moderation. They thus tried to evade
the authority and the importance of the Apostolic Constitutions of Clement XII., Benedict XIV., Pius VII., and Pius IX.
But in the same society there were some who, even against their
own will, acknowledged that the Roman Pontiffs had acted

wisely and lawfully, according to the Catholic discipline. In this many princes and rulers of States agreed with the Popes, and either denounced Masonary to the Apostolic See or by appropriate laws condemned it as a bad thing in Holland, Austria, Switzerland, Spain, Bavaria, Savoy, and other parts of Italy.

But the event justified the prudence of our predecessors, and this is the most important. Nay, their paternal care did not always and everywhere succeed, either bcause of the simulation and shrewdness of the Masons themselves, or through the inconsiderate levity of others whose duty required of them strict attention. Hence, in a century and a half the sect of Masons grew beyond expectation; and, creeping audaciously and deceitfully among the various classes of the people, it grew to be so powerful that now it seems the only dominating power in the States. From this rapid and dangerous growth have come into the Church and into the State those evils which our predecessors had already foreseen. It has indeed come to this, that we have serious fear, not for the Church, which has a foundation too firm for men to upset it, but for those States in which this society is so powerful—or other societies of a like kind, and which show themselves to be servants and companions of Masonry.

For these reasons, when we first succeeded in the government of the Church, we saw and felt very clearly the necessity of opposing so great an evil with the full weight of our authority. On all favorable occasions we have attacked the principal doctrines in which the Masonic perversity appeared. By our Encyclical Letter, *quod apostoloci muneris*, we attack the errors of Socialists and Communists; by the Letter, *Arcanum*, we tried to explain and defend the genuine notion of domestic society, whose source and origin is in marriage; finally, by the letter which begins *Diuturnum*, we proposed a form of civil power consonant with the principles of Christian wisdom, responding to the very nature and to the welfare of people and Princes. Now, after the example of our predecessors, we intend to turn our attention to the Masonic society, to its whole doctrine, to its intentions, acts, and feelings, in order to illustrate more and more this wicked force and stop the spread of this contagious disease.

There are several sects of men which, though different in name, customs, forms, and origin, are identical in aim and sentiment with Masonry. It is the universal center from which they all spring, and to which they all return. Although in our days these seem to no longer care to hide in darkness, but hold their meetings in the full light and under the eyes of their fellow-men and publish their journals openly, yet they deliberate and preserve the habits and customs of secret societies. Nay, there are in them many secrets which are by law carefully concealed not only from the profane, but also from many associated, viz., the last and intimate intentions, the hidden and unknown chiefs, the hidden and secret meetings, the resolutions and methods and means by which they will be carried into execution. Hence the difference of rights and of duties among the members; hence the distinction of orders and grades and the severe discipline by which they are ruled. The initiated must promise ,nay, take an oath, that they will never, at any way or at any time, disclose their fellow-members and the emblems by which they are known, or expose their doctrines. So, by false appearance, but with the same kind of simulation, the Masons chiefly strive, as once did the Manichæans, to hide and to admit no witnesses but their own. They seek skilfully hiding places, assuming the appearance of literary men or philosophers, associated for the purpose of erudition; they have always ready on their tongues the speech of cultivated urbanity, and proclaim their charity toward the poor; they look for the improvement of the masses, to extend the benefits of social comfort to as many of mankind as possible. Those purposes, though they may be true, yet are not the only ones. Besides, those who are chosen to join the society must promise and swear to obey the leaders and teachers with great respect and trust; to be ready to do whatever is told them, and accept death and the most horrible punishment if they disobey. In fact, some who have betrayed the secrets or disobeyed an order are punished with death so skilfully and so audaciously that the murder escaped the investigations of the police. Therefore, reason and truth show that the society of which we speak is contrary to honesty and natural justice.

There are other and clear arguments to show that this society is not in agreement with honesty. No matter how great the skill with which men conceal, it is impossible that the cause should not appear in its effects. "A good tree cannot yield bad fruits, nor a bad tree good ones." (Matt. vii., 18.) Masonry generates bad fruits mixed with great bitterness. From the evidence above mentioned we find its aim, which is the desire of overthrowing all the religious and social orders introduced by Christianity, and building a new one according to its taste, based on the foundation and laws of naturalism.

What we have said or will say must be understood of Masonry in general and of all like societies, not of the individual members of the same. In their number there may be not a few who, though they are wrong in giving their names to these societies, yet are neither guilty of their crimes nor aware of the final goal which they strive to reach. Among the associations also, perhaps, some do not approve the extreme conclusions which, as emanating from common principles, it would be necessary to embrace if their deformity and vileness would not be too repulsive. Some of them are equally forced by the places and times not to go so far as they would go or others go; and yet they are not to be considered less Masonic for that, because the Masonic alliance has to be considered not only from actions and deeds, but from general principles.

Now, it is the principle of naturalists, as the name itself indicates, that human nature and human reason in everything must be our teacher and guide. Having once settled this, they are careless of duties toward God, or they pervert them with false opinions and errors. They deny that anything has been revealed by God; they do not admit any religious dogma and truth but what human intelligence can comprehend; they do not allow any teacher to be believed on his official authority. Now, it being the special duty of the Catholic Church, and her duty only, to keep the doctrines received from God and the authority of teaching with all the heavenly means necessary to salvation and preserve them integrally incorrupt, hence the attacks and rage of the enemies are turned against her.

Now, if one watches the proceedings of the Masons, in respect of religion especially, where they are more free to do what they like, it will appear that they carry faithfully into execution the tenets of the naturalists. They work, indeed, obstinately to the end that neither the teaching nor the authority of the Church may have any influence; and therefore they preach and maintain the full separation of the Church from the State. So law and government are wrested from the wholesome and divine virtue of the Catholic Church, and they want, therefore, by all means to rule States independent of the institutions and doctrines of the Church.

To drive off the Church as a sure guide is not enough; they add persecutions and insults. Full license is given to attack with impunity, both by word and print and teaching, the very foundations of the Catholic religion; the rights of the Church are violated; her divine privileges are not respected. Her action is restricted as much as possible; and that by virtue of laws apparently not too violent, but substantially made on purpose to check her freedom. Laws odiously partial against the clergy are passed so as to reduce its number and its means. The ecclesiastical revenue is in a thousand ways tied up, and religious associations abolished and dispersed.

But the war wages more ardently against the Apostolic See and the Roman Pontiff. He was, under a false pretext, deprived of the temporal power, the stronghold of his rights and of his freedom; he was next reduced to an iniquitous condition, unbearable for its numberless burdens until it has come to this, that the Sectarians say openly what they had already in secret devised for a long time, viz., that the very spiritual power of the Pope ought to be taken away, and the divine institution of the Roman Pontificate ought to disappear from the world. If other arguments were needed for this, it would be sufficiently demonstrated by the testimony of many who often, in times bygone and even lately, declare it to be the real supreme aim of the Freemasons to persecute, with untamed hatred, Christianity, and that they will never rest until they see cast to the ground all religious institutions established by the Pope.

If the sect does not openly require its members to throw away of Catholic faith, this tolerance, far from injuring the Masonic schemes, is useful to them. Because this is, first, an easy way to deceive the simple and unwise ones and it is contributing to proselytize. By opening their gates to persons of every creed they promote, in fact, the great modern error of religious indifference and of the parity of all worships, the best way to annihilate every religion, especially the Catholic, which, being the only true one, cannot be joined with others without enormous injustice.

But naturalists go further. Having entered, in things of greatest importance, on a way thoroughly false, through the weakness of human nature or by the judgment of God, who punishes pride, they run to extreme errors. Thus the very truths which are known by the natural light of reason, as the existence of God, the spirituality and immortality of the soul, have no more consistence and certitude for them.

Masonry breaks on the same rocks by no different way. It is true, Freemasons generally admit the existence of God; but they admit themselves that this persuasion for them is not firm, sure. They do not dissimulate that in the Masonic family the question of God is a principle of great discord; it is even known how they lately had on this point serious disputes. It is a fact that the sect leaves to the members full liberty of thinking about God whatever they like, affirming or denying His existence. Those who boldly deny His existence are admitted as well as those who, like the Pantheists, admit God but ruin the idea of Him, retaining an absurd caricature of the divine nature, destroying its reality. Now, as soon as this supreme foundation is pulled down and upset, many natural truths must need go down, too, as the free creations of this world, the universal government of Providence, immortality of soul, fixture, and eternal life.

Once having dissipated these natural principles, important practically and theoretically, it is easy to see what will become of public and private morality. We will not speak of supernatural virtues, which, without a special favor and gift of God, no one can practice nor obtain, and of which it is impossible to find a vestige in those who proudly ignore the redemption of mankind, heavenly grace, the sacraments, and eternal happiness. We speak of duties which proceed from natural honesty. Because the principles and sources of justice and morality are these, a God, creator and provident ruler of the world, the eternal law which commands respect and forbids the violation of natural order; the supreme end of man settled a great deal above created things outside of this world. These principles once taken away by the Freemasons as by the naturalists, immediately natural ethics has no more where to build or to rest. The only morality which Freemasons admit, and by which they would like to bring up youth, is that which they call civil and independent, or the one which ignores every religious idea. But how poor, uncertain, and variable at every breath of passion is this morality, is demonstrated by the sorrowful fruits which partially already appear. Nay, where it has been freely dominating, having banished Christian education, probity and integrity of manners go down, horrible and monstrous opinions raise their head, and crimes grow with fearful audacity. This is deplored by everybody, and by those who are compelled by evidence and yet would not like to speak so.

Besides, as human nature is infected by original sin and more inclined to vice than to virtue, it is not possible to lead an honest life without mortifying the passions and submitting the appetites to reason. In this fight it is often necessary to despise created good, and undergo the greatest pains and sacrifices in order to preserve to conquering reason its own empire. But naturalists and Masons, rejecting divine revelation, deny original sin, and do not acknowledge that our free will is weakened and bent to evil. To the contrary, exaggerating the strength and excellency of nature, and settling in her the principles and unique rule of justice, they cannot even imagine how, in order to counteract its motions and moderate its appetites, continuous efforts are needed and the greatest constancy. This is the reason why we see so many enticements offerd to the passions, journals, and reviews without any shame, theatrical plays thoroughly dishonest; the liberal arts cultivated according to the principles of an impudent realism, effeminate and delicate living promoted by the most refined inventions; in a word, all the enticements apt to seduce or weaken virtue carefully practiced—things highly to blame, yet becoming the theories of those who take away from man heavenly goods, and put all happiness in transitory things and bind it to earth.

What we have said may be confirmed by things of which it is not easy to think or to speak. As these shrewd and malicious men do not find more servility and docility than in souls already broken and subdued by the tyranny of the passions, there have been in the Masonic sect some who openly said and proposed that the multitudes should be urged by all means and artifice into license, so that they should afterward become an easy instrument for the most daring enterprise.

For domestic society the doctrine of almost all naturalists is that marriage is only a civil contract, and may be lawfully broken by the will of the contracting parties; the State has power over the matrimonial bond. In the education of the children no religion must be applied, and when grown up every one will select that which he likes.

Now Freemasons accept these principles without restriction; and not only do they accept them, but they endeavor to act so as to bring them into moral and practical life. In many countries which are professedly Catholic, marriages not celebrated in the civil form are considered null; elsewhere laws allow divorce. In other places everything is done in order to have it permitted. So the nature of marriage will be soon changed and reduced to a temporary union, which can be done and undone at pleasure.

The sect of the Masons aims unanimously and steadily also at the possession of the education of children. They understand that a tender age is easily bent, and that there is no more useful way of preparing for the State such citizens as they wish. Hence, in the instruction and education of children, they do not leave to the ministers of the Church any part either in directing or watching them. In many places they have gone so far that children's education is all in the hands of laymen: and from moral teaching every idea is banished of those holy and great duties which bind together man and God.

The principles of social science follow. Here naturalists teach that men have all the same rights, and are perfectly equal in condition; that every man is naturally independent; that no one has a right to command others; that it is tryanny to keep men subject to any other authority than that which emanates from themselves. Hence the people are sovereign; those who rule have no authority but by the commission and concession of the people; so that they can be deposed, willing or unwilling, according to the wishes of the people. The origin of all rights and civil duties is in the people or in the State, which is ruled according to the new principles of liberty. The State must be godless; no reason why one religion ought to be preferred to another; all to be held in the same esteem.

Now it is well known that Freemasons approve these maxims, and that they wish to see governments shaped on this pattern and model needs no demonstration. It is a long time, indeed, that they have worked with all their strength and power openly for this, making thus an easy way for those, not a few, more audacious and bold in evil, who meditate the communion and equality of all goods after having swept away from the world every distinction of social goods and conditions.

From these few hints it is easy to understand what is the Masonic sect and what it wants. Its tenets contradict so evidently human reason that nothing can be more perverted. The desire of destroying the religion and Church established by God, with the promise of immortal life, to try to revive, after eighteen centuries, the manners and institutions of paganism, is great foolishness and bold impiety. No less horrible or unbearable is it to repudiate the gifts granted through His adversaries. In this foolish and ferocious attempt, one recognizes that untamed hatred and rage of revenge kindled against Jesus Christ in the heart of Satan.

The other attempt in which the Masons work so much, viz., to pull down the foundations of morality, and become co-operators of those who, like brutes, would see that become lawful which they like, is nothing but to urge mankind into the most abject and ignominious degradation.

This evil is aggravated by the dangers which threaten domestic and civil society. As we have at other times explained, there is in marriage, through the unanimous consent of nations and of ages, a sacred and religious character; and by divine law the conjugal union is indissoluble. Now, if this union is dissovled, if divorce is juridically permitted, confusion and discord must inevitably enter the domestic sanctuary, and woman will lose her dignity and children every security of their own welfare.

That the State ought to profess religious indifference and neglect God in ruling society, as if God did not exist, is a foolishness unknown to the very heathen, who had so deeply rooted in their mind and in their heart, not only the idea of God, but the necessity also of a public worship, that they supposed it to be easier to find a city without any foundation than without any God. And really human society, from which nature has made us, was instituted by God, the author of the same nature, and from Him emanates, as from its source and principle, all this everlasting abundance of numberless goods. As, then, the voice of nature tells us to worship God with religious piety, because we have received from Him life and the goods which accompany life, so, for the same reasons, people and States must do the same. Therefore those who want to free society from any religious duty are not only unjust but unwise and absurd.

Once grant that men through God's will are born for civil society, and that sovereign power is so strictly necessary to society that when this fails society necessarily collapses, it follows that the right of command emanates from the same principle from which society itself emanates; hence the reason why the minister of God is invested with such authority. Therefore, so far as it is required from the end and nature of human society, one must obey lawful authority as we would obey the authority of God, supreme ruler of the universe; and it is a capital error to grant to the people full power of shaking off at their own will the yoke of obedience.

Considering their common origin and nature, the supreme end proposed to every one, and the right and duties emanating from it, men no doubt are all equal. But as it is impossible to find in them equal capacity, and as through bodily or intellectual strength one differs from others, and the variety of customs, inclinations, and personal qualities are so great, it is absurd to pretend to mix and unify all this and bring in the order of civil life a rigorous and absolute equality. As the perfect constitution of the human body results from the union and harmony of different parts, which differ in form and uses, but united and each in his own place form an organism beautiful, strong, useful, and necessary to life, so in the State there is an infinite variety of individuals who compose it. If these all equalized were to live each according to his own whim, it would result in a city monstrous and ugly; whereas if distinct in harmony, in degrees of offices, or inclinations of arts, they co-operate together to the common good, they will offer the image of a city well harmonized and conformed to nature.

The turbulent errors which we have mentioned must inspire governments with fear; in fact, suppose the fear of God in life and respect for divine laws to be despised, the authority of the rulers allowed and authorized would be destroyed, rebellion would be left free to popular passions, and universal revolution and subversion must necessarily come. This subversive revolution is the deliberate aim and open purpose of the numerous communistic and socialistic associations. The Masonic sect has no reason to call itself foreign to their purpose, because Masons promote their designs and have with them common capital principles. If the extreme consequences are not everywhere reached in fact, it is not the merit of the sect nor owing to the will of the members, but of that divine religion which cannot be extinguished, and of the most select part of society, which, refusing to obey secret societies, resists strenuously their immoderate efforts.

May Heaven grant that universally from the fruits we may judge the root, and from impending evil and threatening dangers we may know the bad seed! We have to fight a shrewd enemy, who, cajoling Peoples and Kings, deceives them all with false promises and fine flattery.

Freemasons, insinuating themselves under pretence of friendship into the hearts of Princes, aim to have them powerful aids and accomplices to overcome Christianity, and in order to excite them more actively they calumniate the Church as the enemy of royal privileges and power. Having thus become confident and sure, they get great influence in the government of States, resolve yet to shake the foundations of the thrones, and persecute, calumniate, or banish those sovereigns who refuse to rule as they desire.

By these arts flattering the people, they deceive them. Proclaiming all the time public prosperity and liberty; making multitudes believe that the Church is the cause of the iniquitous servitude and misery in which they are suffering, they deceive people and urge on the masses craving for new things against both powers. It is, however, true that the expectations of hoped-for advantages is greater than the reality; and poor people, more and more oppressed, see in their misery those comforts vanish which they might have easily and abundantly found in organized Christian society. But the punishment of the proud, who rebel against the order established by the providence of God, is that they find oppression and misery exactly where they expected prosperity according to their desire.

Now, if the Church commands us to obey before all God, the Lord of everything, it would be an injurious calumny to believe her the enemy of the power of Princes and a usurper of their rights. She wishes, on the contrary, that what is due to civil power may be given to it conscientiously. To recognize, as she does, the divine right of command, concedes great dignity to civil power, and contributes to conciliate the respect and love of subjects. A friend of peace and the mother of concord, she embraces all with motherly love, intending only to do good to men. She teaches that justice must be united with clemency, equity with command, law with moderation, and to respect every right, maintain order and public tranquility, relieve as much as possible public and private miseries. "But," to use the words of St. Augustine, "they believe, or want to make believe, that the doctrine of Gospel is not useful to society, because they wish that the State shall rest not on the solid foundation of virtue, but on impunity of vice."

It would, therefore, be more according to civil wisdom and more necessary to universal welfare that Princes and Peoples, instead of joining the Freemasons against the Church, should unite with the Church to resist the Freemasons' attacks.

At all events, in the presence of such a great evil, already too much spread, it is our duty, venerable brethren, to find a remedy. And as we know that in the virtue of divine religion, the more hated by Masons as it is the more feared, chiefly consists the best and most solid of efficient remedy, we think that against the common enemy one must have recourse to this wholesome strength.

We, by our authority, ratify and confirm all things which the Roman Pontiffs, our predecessors, have ordered to check the purposes and stop the efforts of the Masonic sect, and all these which they establish to keep off or withdraw the faithful from such societies. And here, trusting greatly to the good will of the faithful, we pray and entreat each of them, as they love their own salvation, to make it a duty of conscience not to depart from what has been on this point prescribed by the Apostolic See.

We entreat and pray you, venerable brethren, who co-operate with us, to root out this poison, which spreads widely among the Nations. It is your duty to defend the glory of God and the salvation of souls. Keeping before your eyes those two ends, you shall lack neither in courage nor in fortitude. To judge which may be the more efficacious means to overcome difficulties and obstacles belongs to your prudence. Yet as we find it agreeable to our ministry to point out some of the most useful means, the first thing to do is to strip from the Masonic sect its mast and show it as it is, teaching orally and by pastoral letters the people about the frauds used by these societies to flatter and entice, the perversity of its doctrines, and the dishonesty of its works. As our predecessors have many times declared, those who love the Catholic faith and their own salvation must be sure that they cannot give their names for any reason to the Masonic sect without sin. Let no one believe a simulated honesty. It may seem to some that Masons never impose anything openly contrary to faith or to morals, but as the scope and nature is essentially bad in these sects, it is not allowed to give one's name to them or to help them in any way.

It is also necessary with assiduous sermons and exhortations to arouse in the people love and zeal for religious instruction. We recommend, therefore, that by appropriate declarations, orally and in writing, the fundamental principles of those truths may be explained in which Christian wisdom is entertained. It is only thus that minds can be cured by instruction, and warned against the various forms of error and vice, and the various enticements especially in this great freedom of writing and great desire of learning.

It is a laborious work, indeed, in which you will have associated and companioned your clergy, if properly trained and taught by your zeal. But such a beautiful and important cause requires the co-operating industry of those laymen who unite doctrine and probity with the love of religion and of their country. With the united strength of these two orders endeavor, dear brethren, that men may know and love the Church; because the more their love and knowledge of the Church grows the more they will abhor and fly from secret societies.

Therefore, availing ourselves of this present occasion, we remind you of the necessity of promoting and protecting the Third Order of St. Francis, whose rules, with prudent indulgence, we lately mitigated. According to the spirit of its institution it intends only to draw men to imitate Jesus Christ, to love the Church, and to practice all Christian virtues, and therefore it will prove useful to extinguish the contagion of sects.

May it grow more and more, this holy congregation, from which, among others, can be expected also this precious fruit of bringing minds back to liberty, fraternity, and equality; not those which are the dream of the Masonic sect, but which Jesus Christ brought into this world and Francis revived. The liberty, we say, of the children of God which frees from the servitude of Satan and from the passions, the worst tyrants; the fraternity which emanates from God, the Father and Creator of all; the equality established on justice and charity, which does not destroy among men every difference, but which, from variety of life, offices, and inclinations, makes that accord and harmony which is exacted by nature for the utility and dignity of civil society.

Thirdly, there is an institution wisely created by our forefathers, and by lapse of time abandoned, which in our days can be used as a model and form for something like it. We mean the colleges or corporations of arts and trades associated under the guidance of religion to defend interests and manners, which colleges, in long use and experience, were of great advantage to our fathers, and will be more and more useful to our age, because they are suited to break the power of the sects. Poor workingmen, for besides their condition, deserving charity and relief, they are particularly exposed to the seductions of the fraudulent and deceivers. They must, therefore, be helped with the greatest generosity and invited to good societies that they may not be dragged into bad ones. For this reason we would like very much to see everywhere arise, fit for the new times, under the auspices and patronage of the Bishops, these associations, for the benefit of the people. It gives us a great pleasure to see them already established in many places, together with the Catholic patronages; two institutions which aim to help the honest class of workingmen, and to help and protect their families, their children, and keep in them, with the integrity of manners, love of piety and knowledge of religion.

Here we cannot keep silence concerning the society of St. Vincent de Paul, celebrated for the spectacle and example offered and so well deserving of the poor. The works and intentions of that society are well known. It is all for the succor and help of the suffering and poor, encouraging them with wonderful tact and that modesty which the less showy the more is fit for the exercise of Christain charity and the relief of human miseries.

Fourthly, in order more easily to reach the end, we recommend to your faith and watchfulness the youth, the hope of civil society. In the good education of the same place a great part of your care. Never believe you have watched or done enough in keeping youth from those masters from whom the contagious breath of the sect is to be feared. Insist that parents and spiritual directors in teaching the catechism may never cease to admonish appropriately children and pupils of the wicked nature of these sects, that they may also learn in time the various fraudulent arts which their propagators use to entice people. Those who prepare children for first communion will do well if they will persuade them to promise not to give their names to any society without asking their parents' or their pastor's or their confessor's advice.

But we understand how our common labor would not be sufficient to outroot this dangerous seed from the field of the Lord, if the Heavenly Master of the vineyard is not to this effect granting to us His generous help. We must, then, implore His powerful aid with anxious fervor equal to the gravity of the danger and to the greatness of the need. Inebriated by its prosperous success, Masonry is insolent, and seems to have no more limits to its pertinacity. Its sectaries bound by an iniquitous alliance and secret unity of purpose, they go on hand in hand and encourage each other to dare more and more for evil. Such a strong assault requires a strong defense. We mean that all the good must unite in a great society of action and prayers. We ask, therefore, from them two things: On one hand, that, unanimously and in thick ranks, they resist immovably the growing impetus of the sects; on the other, that, raising their hands with many sighs to God, they implore that Christianity may grow vigorous; that the Church may recover her necessary liberty; that wanderers may come again to salvation; that errors give place to truth and vice to virtue.

Let us invoke for this purpose the mediation of Mary, the Virgin Mother of God, that against the impious sects in which one sees clearly revived the contumacious pride, the untamed perfidy, the simulating shrewdness of Satan, she may show her power, she who triumphed over him since the first conception.

Let us pray also St. Michael, the prince of the angelic army, conqueror of the infernal enemy; St. Joseph, spouse of the most Saintly Virgin, heavenly and wholesome patron of the Catholic Church; the great Apostles Peter and Paul, propagators and defenders of the Christian faith. Through their patronage and the perseverance of common prayers let us hope that God will condescend to piously help human society threatened by so many dangers.

As a pledge of heavenly graces and of our benevolence, we impart with great affection to you, venerable brethren, to the clergy and people trusted to your care, the Apostolic benediction.

Given at Rome, near St. Peter, the 20th of April, 1884, the seventh year of our pontificate.

LEO, PP. XIII.

A REPLY

FOR

THE ANCIENT AND ACCEPTED SCOTTISH RITE

OF

FREE-MASONRY

TO

THE LETTER "HUMAN GENUS"

OF

POPE LEO XIII.

———

GR.˙. ORIENT OF CHARLESTON.

1884

PRAELOCUTION.

[*From the Allocution of the Grand Commander of the Supreme Council of the 33d Degree for the Southern Jurisdiction of the United States of America.*]

[Delivered in October, 1884, in Supreme Council.]

If the Encyclical Letter of Leo XIII., entitled, from the opening words, "HUMANUM GENUS," had been nothing more than a denunciation of Freemasonary, I should not have thought it worth replying to. But under the guise of a condemnation of Freemasonry, and a recital of the enormities and immoralities of the Order in some respects so absurdly false as to be ludicrous, notwithstanding its malignity, it proved upon perusal to be a declaration of war, and the signal for a crusade, against the rights of men individually and of communities of men as organisms; against the separation of Church and State, and the confinement of the Church within the limits of its legitimate functions; against education free from sectarian religious influences; against the civil policy of non-Catholic countries in regard to marriage and divorce; against the great doctrine upon which, as upon a rock not to be shaken, the foundations of our Republic rest, that "men are superior to institutions. and not institutions to men;" against the right of the people to depose oppressive, cruel and worthless rulers; against the exercise of the rights of free thought and free speech, and against, not only republican, but all constitutional government.

It was the signal for the outbreaking of an already organized conspiracy against the peace of the world, the progress of intellect, the emancipation of humanity, the immunity of human creatures from arrest, imprisonment, torture, and murder by arbitrary power, the right of men to the free pursuit of happiness. It was a declaration of war, arraying all faithful Catholics in the United States not only against their fellow-citiznes, the Brethren of the Order of Freemasons, but against the principles that are the very life-blood of the government of the people of which they were supposed to be a part, and not the members of Italian Colonies, docile and obedient subjects of a foreign Potentate, and of the Cardinals, European and American, his Princes of the Church.

Therefore, seeing it nowhere replied to in the English language in a manner that seemed to me worthy of Freemasonry, I undertook to answer it for the Ancient and Accepted Scottish Rite, which has been ever prompt to vindicate itself from aspersion, and carry the war into the quarters of error. I did not propose to stand upon the defensive, portesting against the accusations of the Papal Bull, as unjust to the Freemasonry of the English-speaking countries of the world, pleading the irresponsibility of British and American Masonry for the acts or opinions of the Freemasonry of the Continent of Europe; nor was I inclined to apologize for the audacity of Freemasonry in daring to exist and to be on the side of the great principles of free government.

When the journal in London which speaks for the Freemasonary of the Grand Lodge of England, deprecatingly protested that the English Masonry was innocent of the charges preferred by the Papal Bull against Freemasonry as one and indivisible; when it declared that the English Freemasonry had no opinions, political or religious, and that it did not in the least degree sympathize with the loose opinions and extravagant utterances of part of the Continental Freemasonry, it was very justly and very conclusively checkmated by the Romish organs with the reply: "It is idle for you to protest. You are Freemasons, and you recognize them as Freemasons. You give them countenance, encouragement and support, and you are jointly responsible with them and cannot *shirk* that responsibility."

And here is what is said by the Bishop of Ascalon, Vivar-Apostolic of Bombay, etc., in a pastoral letter promulgating the Bull.

"In the performance of their duty, the Parish Priests and Confessors must not admit as valid or reasonable the common excuse that Freemasonry in India and England aims at nothing but social amusement, mutual advancement, and charitable benevolence. Such objects require neither a terrible oath of secrecy nor an elaborate system and scale of numerous Degrees, nor a connection with the Masonic Lodges of other countries, about whose anti-Catholic, anti-social, and revolutionary character and aim no doubt nor further concealment is possible. The Masonic Lodges all over the world are firmly knitted and bound together in solidarity. If all of them share in the pleasure of a triumph achieved by a particular Lodge, or by the Lodges of a particular country, all must likewise submit to the Stigma of an anti-Christian, anti-social, and revolutionary sect, as which Freemasonry is in many countries already openly known, and even unblushingly confessed by its own adepts."

I was not willing that the Ancient and Accepted Scottish Rite in the Southern Jurisdiction of the United States should humiliate itself to as little purpose; nor was there any danger that it would do so.

The organs of our American Masonry were inclined to treat the Encyclical Letter as needing no reply, and to regard it with contemptuous indifference. In their opinion, it seemed, the lightnings of the Vatican were harmless, and the American Masonry would do a foolish thing to pay any attention to the Bull. It may be so; and I receive with due humility the admonition that to reply to it was to make much ado about nothing.

But the Freemasonry of the United States is not what it was in the days of the Fathers. While it has succeeded, obedient to the impulsion of Bro. ∴ Richard Vaux, of Pennsylvania, and others, in pretty effectually isolating itself from the Masonry of the rest of the world, other Orders at home unceremoniously jostle it in the struggle for precedence, and it in vain appeals to its antiquity and former prestige to protect it against irreverence. Incalculable harm is being done by Bodies of base origin, whose agents traverse the country soliciting men to receive the counterfeit Degrees which they peddle, selling them by the score for ten or fifteen dollars to anyone who will buy and conferring all in an hour or so, or by administering a single obligation. Rites without claim to be Masonic, teaching nothing worth nothing, flauntingly advertise their multitudes of Degrees that are nothing but numbers and names; new Orders called Masonic spring up like mushrooms; and even the legitimate Masonry, held responsible for all these nuisances and vagaries, parades its uniforms and gewgaws, collars and jewels, too much in the public view, and has so gained popularity while losing its right to reverence.

Its complacent sense of security may be rudely disturbed by and by. It seems to me that an organized crusade against it by all the Roman Catholics in the United States, an anti-Masonic movement organized and directed by the Papacy, and engineered by Priests, Bishops, and Cardinals, is not a thing to be made light of by the American Masonry, treated with indifference and regard with a lordly and sublime contempt. And it is very certain that its protestations that it has no political or religious opinions, and no sympathies with the revolutionary tendencies of the Masonry of the Continent, will neither placate the Papacy nor win for it respect anywhere.

If, in other countries, Freemasonry has lost sight of the Ancient Landmarks, even tolerating communism and atheism, it is better to endure ten years of these evils than it would be to live a week under the devilish tryanny of the Inquisition and of the black soldiery, of Loyola. Atheism is a dreary unbelief, but it at least does not persecute, torture, or roast men who believe that there is a God. Freemasonry will not long indulge in extravagances of opinion or action anywhere. It has within itself the energy and capacity to free itself in time of all errors; and he greatly belittles Humanity who proclaims it to be unsafe to let Error say what it will, if Truth is free to combat and confute it. But Freemasonry will effect its reforms in its own proper way; and would not resort, if it could, not even to save itself from dissolution, to means like those which the Papacy has heretofore employed, and would gladly employ again to extirpate Judaism, Heresy and Freemasonry.

Nowhere in the world has Freemasonry ever conspired against any Government entitled to its obedience or to men's respect. Wherever now there is a Constitutional Government which respects the rights of men and of the people and the public opinion of the world, it is the loyal supporter of that Government. It has never taken pay from armed Despotism, or abetted persecution. It has fostered no Borgias; no stranglers or starvers to death of other Popes, like Boniface VII.; no poisoners, like Alexander VI. and Paul III. It has no roll of beatified Inquisitors or other murderers; and it has never, in any country, been the enemy of the people, the suppressor of scientific truth, the stifler of the God-given right of free inquiry as to the great problems, intellectual and spiritual, presented by the Universe, the extorter of confession by the rack, the burner of women and of the exhumed bodies of the dead. It has never been the enemy of the human race, and the curse and dread of Christendom. Its patron Saints have always been St. John the Baptist and St. John the Evangelist, and not Pedro Arbues d'Epila, Principal Inquisitor of Zaragosa, who, slain in 1485, was beatified by Alexander VII. in 1664.

It is not when the powers of the Papacy are concentrated to crush the Freemasonry of the Latin Kingdoms and Republics of the world, that the Masons of the Ancient and Accepted Scottish Rite in the United States will, from any motive whatever, proclaim that they have no sympathy with the Masons of the Continent of Europe, or with those of Mexico or of the South American Republics. If these fall into errors of practice or indulge in extravagances of dogma, we will dissent and remonstrate; but we will not forget that the Freemasonry of our Rite and of the French Rite has always been the Apostle of Civil and Religious Liberty, and that the blood of Spanish and other Latin Freemasons has again and again glorified and sanctified the implements of torture, the scaffold and the stake, of the Papacy and the Inquisition.

Neither does Freemasonry any more execrate the atrocities of the Papacy than it does those of Henry VIII. of England and his daughter Elizabeth, the murder of Sir Thomas More and that of Servetus, and those of the Quakers put to death by bigotry in New England; than the cruel torturing and slaying of Covenanters and Non-Conformists, the ferocities of Claverhouse and Kirk, and the pitiless slaughtering of Catholic Priests by the revolutionary fury of France.

It well knows and cheerfully acknowledges the services which some of the Roman Pontiffs and a multitude of its clergy have in the past centuries rendered to Humanity. It has always done ample justice to their pure lives, their good deeds, their self-denial, their devotedness, their unostentatious heroism, as these have been eloquently and beautifully protrayed by Kenelm Henry Digby. It has always done full justice to the memories of the faithful and devoted Missionaries of the Order of Jesus and others, who bore the Cross into every barbarous land under the sun, to make known to savages the truths and errors taught by the Roman Church, and the simpler arts of civilization. It was never the unreasoning and insensate reviler of that Church, railing against it without measure or regard to justice and truth; nor could it be, remembering that not only Bayard and Du Guesclin, but Sir Henry More, Las Casas and Fenelon were loyal servants of it.

But also it has known to its cost that none of the pages of the History of the World are more full of frightful crimes and monstrous acts of cruel outrages than those of the Papacy of Rome; and it now knows, by the revival of the Bulls of Benedict and Clement, that the seeming moderation, mildness and liberality of opinion of that Church have been but a mask, which, being torn from its face, its intolerant, persecuting, cruel, inhuman spirit flames out as ferociously as ever from its bloody eyes.

It seems to have learned nothing, and to be incapable of learning anything, although a higher will and a sterner law than its own have made it powerless to burn heretics, whether men or women, free-thinkers and Freemasons, at the stake, or to extort confessions of guilt by torture; and permit it no longer to persecute science as heresy and blasphemy.

For surely if the age of the Papacy had brought with it a larger measure of wisdom, as men were fondly hoping, the present Pope would not, at this age of the world, have ordered every Catholic in very Republic in the world to become not only disloyal to but the irreconcilable enemy of the Government under which he lives.

Nor would the present Pope have re-enacted and made his own the Bulls of Benedict and Clement, or have pronounced against Catholics who persist in continuing to be Freemasons, all the lesser and greater penalties ever prescribed by any of his predecessors. For (not to multiply appalling instances) he cannot be ignorant that, at the first *auto da fe* ("Act of the Faith"), celebrated at Valladolid in Spain, on the 21st of May, 1559, and at the second even more solemn one, held in the same city in the presence of Philip II. himself, his son and sister, the Prince of Parma, and many Grandees and Nobles of Spain and high ladies of the Court and country, there were strangled and then burned, for the unpardonable sin of having become convinced of the truth of, and therefore having embraced, some of the opinions of Martin Luther, Doña Beatrix de Vibero Cazalla and nine other women, in presence of the audience; and at the first, the body of Doña Eleonora de Vibero (who had been interred as a Catholic, without suspicion ever having been raised as to her orthodoxy, and when she had, in her last sickness, taken all the sacraments), having been exhumed, was borne to the pyre on a bier, adorned with a San Benito of flames, the pasteboard mitre on its head, and so burned. Upon the confession extracted from some prisoners under the totures, or by threats of torture, the Fiscal of the Inquisition had accused her, after her burial, of Lutheranism for permitting her home to be used for Lutheran assembings; whereupon she was adjuged by the beloved Tribunal of the Papacy to have died in heresy, her memory was condemned to infamy entailed on her posterity, and her property confiscated, her body ordered to be exhumed and burned, her house razed to the ground and forbidden to be rebuilded and a monument was ordered to be set up on the site with an inscription relating to this event.

Even the impudence of a Roman Catholic journalist will hardly venture to stigmatize this as false. It is related by Juan Antonio Llorente in his "Critical History of the Inquisition in Spain," derived from original documents in the archives of the Supreme Tribunal and those of the Subterranean Tribunals of the Holy Office: from which came the statements contained in our "Reply" of the number of victims butchered by Torquemada and his successors. Llorente was ex-Secretary of the Inquisition of the Court, Canon of the Primatical Church of Toledo, Chancellor of the University of that city, Knight of the Order of Charles III., and member of the Royal Academies of History and of the Spanish Language at Madrid.

"All these dispositions" (of the judgment aaginst the dead woman Eleonora) "were executed," Llorente says: "I have seen the place, the column and the inscriptions. It is stated that this monument of human ferocity against the dead was demolished in 1809."

But at these *auto da fe* the Archbishops and Bishops, clergy, nobles, and ladies present were not entirely deprived of the expected luxury and pleasure of seeing human creatures burned alive. At the first, Francisco de Vibero Cazalla and the Licentiate Antonio Herrezuelo, and at the second, Don Carlos de Seso and Juan Sanchez, were roasted alive for the mortal sin of

Lutheranism. Of a score or two of suspected Lutherans and others, not burned alive, or strangled and then burned, all the property they possessed was confiscated to the uses of the Holy Office, a method of enriching itself which it had then pursued with great diligence, by continual confiscations, for eighty years, and yet was not weary.

At the second, Doña Marina de Guevara, a Nun, accused of Lutheranism, suffered. The Supreme Tribunal decreed that she was guilty, and had incurred the penalty of the grater excommunciation and *"remitted"* her "to the judicial power and to the secular arm" of the Corregidor and his Lieutenant, *"to whom,"* the judgment said, *"we recommend to treat her with kindness and pity,"* that Tribunal knowing that sentence of death must inevitably and necessarily follow, and that its own judgment was really the death sentence. If the Corregidor had dared to mitigate the penalty, he would himself have felt fastened into his flesh the sharp and venomous fangs of the Inquisition, for he would have proven himself a favourer of heretics. What a hideous formula was that recommendation to kindness and pity! "It is impossible," Llorente says, "to impose on God by formulas contrary to the secret dispositions of the heart."

"Since the Inquisition was established," Llorente wrote in 1817, "there has hardly been a man celebrated for his knowledge who has not been persecuted as a heretic;" and he gives a formidable list of those who suffered in their liberty, honour and fortune "because they would not shamefully adopt scholastic opinions or erroneous systems born in the ages of ignorance and of barbarism."

Certainly the restoration of this convenient instrument of the Apostolic See, which acts on anonymous denunciations, takes testimony *ex parte* upon such denunciations, and convicts on suspicions, and confessions extorted by an admirable variety of tortures, and even upon persistent refusals to confess, is not impossible; because, on the 21st of July, 1814, Ferdinand VII. re-established it in Spain, after Bonaparte had suppressed it in 1808, and the Cortes-General Extraordinary of Spain had done the same on the 12th of February, 1813.*

---

*In the Gaceta of the Spanish Government, No. of date 23d February, 1826, the execution of a person accused of Masonry is thus referred to:

"Yesterday was hung in this city Antonio Caso, (alias) *Jaramalla:* he died impenitent, and leaving in consternation the numerous concourse which were present at the spectacle; a terrible whirlwind making it more horrible, which took place while this criminal was expiring, who came forth from the prison blaspheming, speaking such words as may not be repeated without shame, and although gagged he repeated as well as he could, '*Viva mi Secta!   Viva la Institucion Masonical!*' So he was dragged by the tail of a horse to the scaffold. Notwithstanding the efforts which Priests of all classes had made, they had not been able to induce him to pronounce the name of Jesus and Mary. After he was dead, his right hand was cut off, and dragging his body they took it to a dung-heap. Thus do these proclaimers of liberty miserably end their lives; and this is the felicity which they promise to thos who follow them,—to go to abide where the beasts do."

The time may even come again, if Constitutional Government can be destroyed by the Papacy in Spain, Portugal or Italy, when that may happen to a Freemason, which happened to Gaspardo de Santa Cruz and his son under Ferdinand and Isabella, about the year 1487. The father had taken refuge at Toulouse, in France, where he died, after he had been burned in effigy at Zaragoza. One of his sons was arrested by order of the Inquisitors for having aided the escape of his father. He underwent the punishment of the public *auto da fe*, and was condemned to take a copy of the judgment rendered against his father, to go to Toulouse and present this copy to the Dominicans, demanding that his father's body should be exhumed and burned; and, finally, to return to Zaragoza and make report to the Inquisitors of the execution of the sentence. And to this shameful, revolting, and monstrous judgment he submitted without murmuring, and executed it.

In 1524 (Charles V. being then Emperor of the Romans) there was put up, in the Inquisition at Sevilla, by the Licentiate de la Cueva by the order and at the cost of the Emperor, an inscription in Latin, composed by Diego de Cortegana, by which it was stated that, from the time of the establishment of the Inquisition there, in 1485, under the Pontificate of Sextus IV. and during the reign of Fredinand V. and Isabella, until 1524, *"more than two thousand persons obstinate in heresy had been delivered to the flames,* after having been judged conformably to law, with the approbation and favour of Innocent VIII., Alexander VI., Pius III., Julius II., Leo X., Adrian VI., and Clement VII."

The Church of Rome had prepared and matured all its plans of campaign against liberal institutions and Constitutional Government, carefully, thoroughly, and comprehensively, before the Encyclical Letter "Humanum Genus" gave the signal for openin the campaign and commencing the new crusade, to endanger the peace of the world, foment anarchy, and initiate a new era of violence and murder. A clerical victory at the elections in Belgium has been followed by the enactment of a law destructive of the common-school system, and placing education under the control of the Priests and Jesuits. It will not disturb the Pope or his Cardinal-Princes if civil war results, as now seems probable, if thousands of lives are sacrificed, if the King loses his throne, and the Kingdom of Belgium is obliterated. In Spain the Romish clergy have set on foot a demonstration in every Church throughout the realm in favour of the temporal power of the Pope; and if Alfonso does not place himself unreservedly in the hands and at the bidding of the Church, revolutionary movements against his throne, already beginning to appear in the north of Spain will be fomented. The Pope promulgates an Encyclical Letter against the adoption of a new law of divorce by the legislative power of France, and instructs the Bishops to annul it so far as they may find it possible. And we may look for disturbances in Mexico and the South American States, fomented by the Priesthood in obedience to the orders issued from the Vatican against Freemasons and Constitutional Government.

By Papal Brief of Jaunary 17, 1750, the Father Joseph Torrubia, Pro-Censor and Revisor of the Inquisition, was authorized to procure initiation into Masonry, to take all the oaths that might be required of him, and to use every means possible to acquire the most complete knowledge of the membership of the Freemasonry of Spain; and in March, 1751, the Father Torrubia, having taken without sinfulness the oaths required, and been initiated, put into the hands of the Grand Inquisitor the ninety-seven lists of membership of the ninety-seven Lodges at that time in activity in Spain: upon which, on the 2d of July, 1751, the King Ferdinand VI. decreed the complete suppression of the Masonic Order, and prescribed the punishment of death, *without any form of preliminary procedure*, against all who should be convicted of belonging to it.

Undoubtedly Pope Leo XIII. would consider it laudable for any good Catholic now, if need were, to imitate the example of the Father Joseph Torrubia; and entirely proper for himself to grant such a brief as was granted to that worthy Father; although all honest men ought to regard such a service as base and infamous, and consider perjury and betrayal of confidence to be virtues only in the eyes of the Church and not in those of God.

But his Apostolic Holiness has graciously permitted that during one year, those who in obedience to his orders renounce Masonry, shall not be required to divulge the names of their superiors in the Order;—not because to do so would be unutterable baseness, but because it is polite, as likely to induce many to renounce the Order, who would not be willing to do that and at the same time become faithless and perjured scoundrels.

While inciting the fanatical and venal instruments of his Priesthood against Freemasonry and Constitutional Government, the Pope omits nothing to make more effectual his edict of Excommunication. It is necessary to give assurance to those who may help in the good work of exterminating Freemasonry, overturning Constitutional Government, and re-enslaving intellects, souls and science, of immunity, if not in this world, then certainly in the next, for all the outrages, villainies and crimes that they may commit.

Accordingly the Pope embraces the present occasion, while he is causing disturbances in Belgium, Spain, Mexico and Italy, to issue his proclamation, as Spiritual Autocrat of the whole world, panoplied with all the powers of the Almighty God, by which he plenarily pardons all the sins of a great number of the faithful, neither knowing nor caring what the enormity of those sins may be.

The paragraphs which follow, taken from a translation in the Catholic Examiner of Brooklyn, of the Encyclical Letter of Leo XIII., of August 30, 1884, "setting apart October as a month of prayer to the Mother of God," will show that we do not misunderstand the use to which the Pope puts his plenary indulgences. The italics are ours:

"For it is, indeed, an arduous and exceedingly weighty matter that is now in hand; *it is to humiliate an old and most subtle enemy in the spread-out array of his power;* to win back the freedom of the Church and of her Head; to preserve and secure the fortifications within which should rest in peace the safety and weal of human society.

    *   *   *   *   *   *   *

"That the heavenly treasures of the Church may be thrown open to all, we hereby renew every indulgence granted by us last year. To all those, therefore, who shall have assisted on the prescribed days at the public recital of the Rosary, *and have prayed for our intentions;* to all those, also, who from legitimate causes shall have been compelled to do so in private, we grant for each occasion an indulgence of seven years and seven times forty days. To those who, in the prescribed space of time, shall have performed these devotions at least ten times—either publicly in the churches or from just causes in the privacy of their homes—and shall have expiated their sins by confession and have received communion at the altar, we grant from the treasury of the Church a plenary indulgence. We also grant this full forgiveness of sins and plenary remission of punishment to all those who, either on the feast-day itself of our Blessed Lady of the Rosary, or on any day within the subsequent eight days, shall have washed the stains from their souls and have holily partaken of the Divine banquet, *and shall have also prayed in any church to God and His holy Mother for our intentions.*"

What these "intentions" are, the Letter HUMANUM GENUS does not permit the world to doubt. And in the latest Encyclical Letter, granting absolutions in advance, they are expressed in this sentenc:

"May our Heavenly Patroness, invoked by us through the Rosary, graciously be with us and obtain that, all disagreements of opinion being removed and Christianity restored through the world, we may obtain from God the wished for peace in the Church."

It is also proclaimed that another letter is about to be issued which will cause a profound sensation in the Catholic world, in which the Pope is to expound to his vassals his opinions in regard to civil government. He cannot make them much more plain than he has already made them; but it is not probable that his lofty intentions will be in any degree abated. He has already proclaimed war against Protestantism, free education, and constitutional restraints upon arbitrary power; and he will continue to do so more and more emphatically and offensively, until not only the rulers of Protestant countries, but all, wherever constitutional government exists, will find themselves compelled to declare the Papacy the malignant disturber of the peace of the world, and to unite in measures to curb its arrogance and deprive it of the power of making mischief and of its cherished prerogative of being the curse and the terror of the world.

Freemasonry makes no war upon the Roman Catholic religion. To do this is impossible for it, because it has never ceased to proclaim its cardinal tenets to be the most perfect and absolute equality of right of free opinion in matters of faith and creed. It denies the right of one Faith to *tolerate* another. To tolerate is to permit; and to permit is to refrain from prohibiting or preventing; and so a right to tolerate would imply a right to forbid. If there be a right to tolerate, every Faith has it alike. One is in no wise, in the eye of Masonry, superior to the other, and of two opposing faiths each cannot be superior to the other, nor can each tolerate the other.

Rome does claim the right to prohibit, precisely now as she always did. She is never tolerant except upon compulsion. And Masonry, having nothing to say as to her religious tenets denies her right to interfere with the free exercise of opinion.

It will be said that the English-speaking Freemasonry will not receive Catholics into its bosom. That is not true. It will not receive Jesuits, because no oath that it can administer would bind the conscience of a Jesuit; and it refuses also to receive Atheists; not denying their perfect right to be atheists, but declining to accept them for associates, because Masonry recognizes a Supreme Will, Wisdom and Power, a God, who is a protecting Providence to whom it is not folly to pray, and who has not made persecution a religious duty, nor savage cruelty and blood-guiltiness a passport to Paradise.

A REPLY

OF

FREEMASONRY IN BEHALF OF HUMANITY

TO

THE ENCYCLICAL LETTER "HUMANUM GENUS"

OF

THE POPE LEO XIII.

FROM THE GRAND ORIENT OF CHARLESTON IN THE STATE OF SOUTH CAROLINA.

THE SUPREME COUNCIL OF THE 33D DEGREE OF THE ANCIENT AND ACCEPTED SCOTTISH RITE OF FREEMASONRY, FOR THE SOUTHERN JURISDICTION OF THE UNITED STATES OF AMERICA:

BY THE GRAND COMMANDER:

To the Brethren of our Obedience throughout all our Jurisdiction:

∴שׁ   ∴שׁ   ∴שׁ

It is known unto you that Leo XIII., at present the Pope of the Roman Catholic Church, claiming to be the successor of Saint Peter the Apostle, infallible, and the Vicegerent of God, has lately issued an Encyclical Letter to the Catholic World, to be known hereafter, from the words with which it begins, as the Letter HUMANUM GENUS, in calumnious denunciation of Freemasonry and Freemasons.

The Ancient and Accepted Scottish Rite of Freemasonry, which, a century and more ago, accepted the Apostolate of Civil and Religious Liberty, and hath, since then, not faltered in its purpose of making these as common among men as light and air, has not thought it necessary to be in haste, here in the United States, to make reply to the Bull of Excommunication of the Roman Pontiff; because it finds, in the Letter itself, the most sufficient proof that it does not need to feel any fear for the result of the long controversy which, forced by the Church of Rome, by its Jesuit soldiery and by its bloody and ferocious Tribunals of the Holy Office, on long-suffering Humanity, has brought upon itself signal discomfiture, with immense loss of temporal and spiritual power.

Least of all will it, now or at any time, or anywhere, seek to conciliate the Church of Rome, or to plead in avoidance of its denunciations, that it does not in any wise intermeddle or concern itself with questions of civil government or religion. It leaves that to those Bodies and Journals, to which it may seem advisable or expedient, reminding them that it long ago said to them this, which it may now be profitable for them to ponder upon:

"In *this* Freemasonry we do not disclaim all the attributes that once distinguished the Order, except a portion of its morality; nor protest against the suspicion that it has a political and religious creed, as though it were an accusation of crime. It is not a negative but a positive Institution, that does not rely upon the insignificance of its objects to make it sufficiently contemptible not to excite the fears of Emperors and Kings. The sedulous disclaimer by English and German Masonry, and very recently by that of France, of all pretence to religious or political principle, has not averted the thunderbolts of the Vatican, and the humiliation has, so far, been fruitless."

But it is the right of the Ancient and Accepted Scottish Freemasonry to make answer if it sees fit, and to carry the war into the quarters of error, however willing it might be to leave the Encyclical Letter to have its effect, and work to the Church of Rome all the harm it may, without comment. It neither fears the Pontiff, nor concerns itself about his vituperations; and it could do itself, and the great cause in which it is enlisted, sufficient service, perhaps, by republishing the Letter, and giving to it as wide publicity as possible.

We will probably do that hereafter; as we have already, some years ago, published in full translations of the equally formidable Bulls of the Predecessors, Clement and Benedict, of the present Pope. Neither should we be concerned if it were to be thought, by the outside world, in case we should remain silent, that our Freemasonry is afraid to reply, or feels that it cannot efficiently defend itself. But, as it seems to be considered by many of you, our very dear Brethren, that we ought to make answer for you, we willingly undertake to do so, for ourselves and you, and for our Freemasonry, so far as we may have authority to speak for it.

In doing this we shall not set forth the whole Letter, nor quote from it at very great length; but only so far as it may be necessary to set its words forth, to enable you and others who may read what we write, to see against what it in reality is that the Church of Rome launches its no longer formidable lightnings.

In its long war against Humanity and human progress, against Science and Civilization, and against the truth of God revealed in Nature, the Roman Church has been greatly shorn of power and influence, until it has become but the feeble effigy of what it was in 1483, when it made Tomas Torquemada Inquisitor of the Faith in Spain, and in the eighteen years of that Official's rule burned at the stake in that Kingdom *eight thousand eight hundred* Hebrews and Heretics.

But the Pope is still a great religious Potentate, wielding an immense influence, especially over ignorance, throughout a large part of Christendom, with an army of over 11,000 Jesuit Fathers, Professors and Coadjutors, of whom there are nearly 2,000 Fathers in England and the United States. While Freemasonry has never feared, it has never undervalued its mighty antagonist, and it does not underestimate him now, although it listens with equanimity to these words, with which his Letter begins:

"THE HUMAN RACE, after its most miserable defection, through the wiles of the Devil, from its Creator, God, the giver of celestial gifts, has divided into two different and opposite factions; of which one fights ever for truth and virtue, the other for their opposites. One is the Kingdom of God on earth, *the true Church of Jesus Christ,* . . . the other is the Kingdom of Satan. . . . But at this time those who support the worst faction seem all to be conspiring and striving most vigorously, *led and aided by what is called Freemasonry,* a society of men most widely spread and firmly established. For now in no way concealing their designs, they are rousing themselves most boldly against the power of God; undisguisedly and openly they are planning destruction for the Holy Church, and they do so with this intention—that they may, if it be possible, completely despoil Christian Nations of the benefits obtained through Jesus Christ our Saviour."

"In so pressing a danger, in so monstrous and obstinate an attack on Christianity, it is Our duty to indicate the peril, to point out Our adversaries, and as far as we can to resist their plans and designs, that those whose safety has been entrusted to Us may not perish everlastingly; and that the Kingdom of Jesus Christ, which We have received to protect, not only may stand and remain unimpaired, but may even be increased throughout the world."

This is clearly a manifesto against every *other* Church, calling itself "Christian," than the Roman-Catholic Church, as no part of "the Kingdom of God upon Earth," of "the true Church of Jesus Christ;" as in no wise dispensing among men "the benefits obtained through Jesus Christ our Saviour." The Pope has alone received "the Kingdom of Jesus Christ" to protect. All so-called "Christianity," except the Roman Church, is "the Kingdom of Satan." Thus this Letter is the shrill and discordant war-cry of Intolerance and of "death to Heresy," sounded from the summit of the Vatican, and echoing and re-echoing over the world.

"Therefore, whatsoever the Popes our Predecessors have decreed to hinder the designs and attempts of the Sect of Freemasons; whatsoever they have ordained to deter or recall persons from Societies of this kind, each and all we do ratify and confirm by our Apostolic Authority."

And these are specially stated to be the Bull *In Eminenti* of Clement XII., dated 27th April, 1738, confirmed and renewed by that beginning *Providas* of Benedict XIV., 17th of May, 1751; the Edict of Pius VII., in 1821, and the Apostolic Edict *Quo Graviora* of Leo XII., in 1825; with those of Pius VII., in 1829, Gregory XVI., in 1832, and Pius IX., in 1846, 1865, etc.

The title of the Bull IN EMINENTI of Clement XII. is "Condemnatio Societatis seu Conventiculorum *de Liberi Muratori*, seu *the Freemasons*, under the penalty *ipso facto* incurred, of excommunication; absolution from it, except *in articulo mortis*, being reserved to the Supreme Pontiff."

Let us give the exact language, translated, of the closing sentences of this celebrated Bull. It will sound strangely, even to Catholics, at this day; but their Spiritual Sovereign has, by plenarily confirming and re-enacting it, made it a part, in the very words, of his Letter Encyclical:

"We will, moreover, and command, that as well Bishops and Superior Prelates, and other Ordinaries of particular places, AS THE INQUISITORS OF HERETICAL PRAVITY UNIVERSALLY DEPUTED, of what State, degree, condition, Order, dignity or pre-eminence soever, PROCEED and INQUIRE, and RESTRAIN and COERCE the same, AS VEHEMENTLY SUSPECTED OF HERESY, WITH CONDIGN PUNISHMENT; for to them and each of them we hereby give and impart free power of PROCEEDING, INQUIRING AGAINST, and of COERCING and RESTRAINING WITH CONDIGN PUNISHMENTS, the same transgressors; AND OF CALLING IN, IF IT SHALL BE NECESSARY, THE HELP OF THE SECULAR ARM. . . . Let no one, therefore, infringe, or by rash attempt contradict, this page of our Declaration, Condemnation, Command, Prohibition and Interdict; but if any one shall presume to attempt this, let him know that he will incur the indignation of Almighty God, and of the blessed Apostles Peter and Paul."

The Bull of Benedict XIV., "BY which," the title reads, "certain Societies or Conventicles, *de Liberi Muratori*, seu *the Freemasons*, or otherwise called, *iterum damnantur et prohibentur*, with invocations of the arm and aid of the Secular Princes and Powers," was issued to remove doubts whether the penalty of excommunication *ipso facto* pronounced by Clement, was still in full force, not having yet been confirmed by Benedict. It prescribed how absolution might be obtained by penitents renouncing Masonry; but incited the competent judges and tribunals to proceed with renewed activity against the violators of that Constitution of Clement, and he confirmed it in its very words, inserting it in full in this his own Bull.

And he specially declared that "among the gravest causes of the aforesaid prohibition and damnation, one is, that in such Societies and Conventicles, men of any Religion and Sect whatsoever do consociate; whereby it sufficiently appears that great mischief to the purity of the Catholic religion may arise."

The Archbishop of Avignon, publishing this Bull on the 22d of July, 1751, to the Clergy and Faithful of his Diocese, required all Freemasons therein to renounce the Order, addressing themselves to him or to the Father Inquisitor or one of the Vicars-General; and specially commanded, on penalty of excommunication, those having possession of a certain manuscript-book, containing the regulations of the Order, and the signatures of those admitted into it, to place it, as soon as possible, in his hands, or those of the Inquisitor; and anyone knowing where it was, to give information thereof. And he said, "If anyone, which God forbid! is blind and hardened enough to still persist in these societies named *Freemasons*, or called by any other name, let him know that we will proceed against him *as suspected of heresy, according to the full rigour of the law.*"

The ratification and full confirmation of everything in these Bulls of Clement and Benedict, formally excommunicates *ipso facto* every Freemason in the world; and, so far as the Pope can do it, releases the people of Germany and Brazil from their allegiance to their Emperors, and those of Sweden and Norway and the Netherlands from their allegiance to their Kings; and, when the Prince of Wales shall become King, will release every Catholic in Great Britain and its colonies from their allegiance.

How fully these excommunications *ipso facto*, and references of cases, as of heretical pravity, to the Inquisition, with power to call on the Secular arm, and light again the fire of Hell on earth at new *Autos da Fé*, are re-enacted by the new Bull HUMANUM GENUS, will fully appear from the words which we next quote:

"Seeing then that the purpose and nature of Freemasonry has been discovered from the clear evidence of facts, from the knowledge of its causes, from the publication of its laws, rites and documents, and from the confirmatory testimony of those who had part in it, this Apostolic See has declared and clearly proclaimed that the Sect of Freemasons, established against law and right, is dangerous no less to Christianity than to the State, *and has proclaimed and ordered,* UNDER THE HEAVIER PENALTIES USED BY THE CHURCH AGAINST THE GUILTY, that no one should be enrolled in that Society."

"And this action of the Popes *seemed to be entirely approved* by many *Princes and rulers* WHOSE CARE IT WAS EITHER TO PROCEED AGAINST THE MASONIC SOCIETY BEFORE THE APOSTOLIC SEE, *or of themselves to condemn them to punishment, by laws passed for this purpose, as in Holland, Austria, Switzerland, SPAIN, Bavaria, Savoy, and other parts of Italy."*

"Proceeding against it before the Apostolic See'—that is, making their subjects victims of the merciless and remorseless Inquisition, in Portugal. "Or by laws passed by themselves, to condemn them to punishment," like that of Ferdinand VII. of Spain, of August 1, 1824—a decree expedited condemning to death all Freemasons who should not declare themselves such within thirty days; after which time all were to be hung within twenty-four hours, *without other form of trial*, who might be recognized as Freemasons, not having so declared themselves.

The Masons of France do not forget that, soon after the Bull *In Eminenti* issued (of April 27, 1738), a French writer on Freemasonry was burned to death at Rome; nor those of Portugal the memorable Bull of 1st September, 1774, which proclaimed and eulogized the services rendered to the Papacy in Portugal, since 1732; viz., that there had been made to do penance in public *Autos* 23,068 persons; that 1,415 had been burned; that 2,000 had been thrown into the Tagus, and more than that number had died in prison; nor those of Spain, that Riego was brutally put to death at Madrid, Palacios at Cadiz, Galvez at Granada, and others in Sevilla and Barcelona, for the sole offense of being Masons.

In 1737, Clement XII. issued an Allocution authorizing the mission of an Inquisitor to Leghorn, because a Lodge there was said to receive Roman Catholics, Protestants and Jews.

It is the crowning glory of Freemasonry that, requiring only that a Candidate shall believe and put his trust in a living and personal God, a beneficent and protecting Providence, to whom it is not folly to pray; and shall believe in the continued existence of the Soul of man after the death of the body, it receives into its Lodges the Christian of every sect, the Hebrew, the Moslem and the Parsee, and unites them in the holy bonds of Brotherhood.

In the eye of the Papacy, it is a crime to belong to an Order which is thus constituted; and this the Letter of the Pope Leo (successor of *"Divus Alexander VI., Iste Deus"*)* preaches to Catholics living in a Republic, the very cornerstone of which is religious toleration, and which was peopled in large measure,

---

*Corius, *in Historid Mediolanense* describes more accurately than any other writer the coronation at Rome in the Church of San Pietro, on the 27th of August, 1492, of Pope ALEXANDER VI. |Rodrigos Borgia, father of Cesar Borgia. When his election was announced, by throwing from the window of the Vatican little strips of paper, with his name as Pope written in Latin on them, and these beginnings, full of a vain ostentation, were observed with astonishment, the Cardinal de Medicis said to Lorenzo Cibo, "Monseigneur, we are delivered over to the gullet of the most voracious wolf that has perhaps ever been in the world, and which will infallibly devour us, if we do not anticipate him by flight."

at first, by Puritans, Quakers, Church-of-England-men and Huguenots.

"Under the heavier penalties used by the Church against the guilty." Yea, under the heaviest; to which, if that Church could do it, it would again resort today. We have seen a Catholic Ultramontane Archbishop in Brazil, within a few years, excommunicate all the Freemasons in his jurisdiction; forbid the administration of the Last Sacraments to Masons dying; forbid their burial in consecrated ground; forbid the Priests to solemnize the Rites of Marriage between a Freemason and any woman, and so compel the Parliament of that Catholic country to make lawful a marriage solemnized by a civil magistrate.

We know what these heavier penalties of the Church were. They are the same as when, at Toledo, in 1486, twenty-seven persons were burned by the Inquisition, chiefly for being Hebrews; and at Seville, in 1481, 2,000, for the same crime— *two thousand* human beings, roasted to death by slow fires, assassinated in the name of a religion of peace;—the same as when, in Spain, from 1481 to 1498, Torquemada burned *eight thousand eight hundred* men and women;—as when his successor, the Dominican Friar Diego Deza, successively Bishop of Samora, Salamanca, Jaen and Palencia, and Archbishop of Sevilla, in eight years, from 1498 to 1506, burned 1,664;—as when his successor, the most celebrated Archbishop of Toledo,

---

On one of the great triumphal arches erected, in letters of gold on a blue ground, was the legend:

VATICINIUM VATICANI IMPERII;

on another part of it,

ALEX. VI. PONT. MAX.;

and on another,

DIVI ALEXANDRI MAGNI CORONATIO.

And on another arch were inscribed the lines, composed by the Protonotary Angello,

"CÆSARE MAGNA FUIT, NUNC ROMA EST MAXIMA, SEXTUS REGNAT ALEXANDER, ILLE VIR, ISTE DEUS;"

"BY CÆSAR ROME WAS GREAT, BUT NOW IS GREATEST: REIGNS ALEXANDER SIXTH: THE FORMER WAS A MAN, THE LATTER IS GOD."

In another verse, it was written,

SCIT VENISSE SUUM PATRIA GRATA JOVEM: THE GRATEFUL COUNTRY KNOWS ITS JOVE HAS COME;

In another,

INVICTOQUE JOVI EST CURA PRIMUS HONOR, TO THE UNCONQUERED JOVE PROTECTION IS THE CHIEFEST HONOUR.

Another verse was,

LIBERTAS, PIA JUSTITIA, ET PAX AUREA, OPES, QUÆ SUNT TIBI, ROMA, NOVUS FUIT DEUS ISTE TIBI.

LIBERTY, PIOUS JUSTICE, GOLDEN PEACE, THE LARGESSES WHICH, ROME! ARE THINE, THIS NEW GOD BRINGS TO THEE.

Petrus Delphinus, who was a spectator, says that he read the inscription "CÆSARE MAGNA FUIT, NUNC ROMA EST MAXIMA: SEXTUS REGNAT ALEXANDER: ILLE VIR, ISTE DEUS," and that he heard it 'not much commended' by many considerable persons.

Cisneros, a Franciscan Brother, from 1507 to 1517, burned 2,536;—as when the Cardinal Adriano, Bishop of Tortosa, succeeding Cisneros as Inquisitor-General, from 1518 to 1522, burned 1,344;—as when the Cardinal Alonso Manrique, Archbishop of Sevilla, succeeding him, from 1523 to 1538, burned 2,350;—as when Taveda, Archbishop of Toledo, succeeding Manrique in 1539, and dying in 1545, burned alive 840;—as when Cardinal Loaisa, General of the Dominicans, Confessor of Charles V., Commissary-General of the Crusade and Archbishop of Sevilla, from the 15th of February, 1546, to the 22nd of April in the same year, burned 120; as when his successor, Fernando Valdés, Archbishop of Sevilla, from 1547 to 1566, burned 2,400;—as when, from 1566 to 1572, Cardinal Espinosa burned 720; and from 1572 to 1594, Pedro de Cordova Ponce de Liano, Bishop of Badajoz, Inquisitor-General, burned 2,816; and Jeronimo de Lara, Bishop of Cartagena, in a few months, 128; from 1596 to 1599, burned 184; and Fernando Niño de Guevara, from 1599 to 1602, burned 240; and Juan de Zuniga, Bishop of Cartagena, in a few months, 80; and Juan Baptista de Azevedo, from 1603 to 1607, 400;—as when, from 1643 to 1665, the Inquisitor-General Diego Arce y Reinoso burned 1,422; and Diego Sarmiento de Valladares, from 1669 to 1699, burned 1,248;—as when, from 1699 to 1720, 884 were burned; and from 1720 to 1733, by the Inquisitor-General Juan de Camargo, 442; 238 from 1733 to 1740; 136 from 1742 to 1745; 10 from 1746 to 1759, and 4 from 1750 to 1783.

As when, in all, from 1481 to 1783, besides the thousands upon thousands murdered by the Inquisition in other ways, *thirty-four thousand six hundred and fifty-six* men and women were *burned to death*, in Spain alone; and 304,451 endured other heavy punishments. What a Devil's Carnival, of the Church that so hates Freemasonry!

Civilized Humanity was successfully endeavoring to forget these and a thousand other atrocities of savage mercilessness that seem to those who have not read history to be incredible and monstrous fictions. It was beginning to believe that the Church, which had during three hundred long years resorted to and availed itself of the methods and practices of its creature, the Holy Office, or Inquisition, had become humanized and enlightened, by the beautiful influences of Science and an immensely larger knowledge of Humanity and of God, acquired by studying the great Book of Nature, His first and absolutely authentic Revelation of Himself. It was believed that the Papal Despotism, Vicegerency of God in its own estimation, would not today, if it had the power, imprison or torture an observer of nature who should deny that, at the command of Joshua, in order to enable the Israelites to slaughter the Amorites satisfactorily, the Sun stood still upon Gideon in the midst of Heaven, and hasted not to go down about a whole day, and the Moon stayed in the Valley of Ajalon. It was not believed that it would now, if it could, visit with "the heaver penalties" a physician who might doubt whether, when Christ abode on earth, Devils found homes somewhere in the interiors of men, and when compelled to vacate these homes, sought new abodes in the swine, grubbing for roots in the arid soil of Galilee.

It was believed that the Church Infallible had at least tacitly relinquished some of the gross absurdities of its old belief, errors and fallacies contradicted and exploded by the revelation of the Creator Himself, made known to men by His hand-maidens, Geology and Palæontology, Chemistry, Astronomy and Dynamics. It was not supposed that, if it still had the power, the Church of Rome would today sentence Darwin and his disciples even to march in procession in an *Auto da Fe* grotesquely clad as heretics, much less burn them alive, as it would with great rejoicing have done three centuries ago.

It was believed that the Pope looked with at least tolerant and indulgent eyes upon the people of the great Protestant Kingdoms and Countries, upon the Clergy and Laity of other denominations of Christians, upon even such Hebrews as Sir Moses Montefiore; felt that the Turk, the Moor, the Parsee or the Hebrew was entitled to somewhat more merciful consideration and greater immunity from torture and mutilation than the dog, the wolf, or the hyena; and no longer considered it to be contrary to the law of God for men to insist upon imposing constitutional restrictions upon Autocracies and Despotisms, and for the Pope to demand to have a voice in the making of laws.

We, here in the United States, fondly believed in the *entente cordiale* between our constitutional Republicanism and the humanized Church of Rome. Free of all apprehension of danger from its ambition, slow to believe that it would gladly, if it could, turn back the hands upon the dial of Time, rob Humanity here of all the civil, political and religious rights which it has acquired in the long and bloody struggle of ages against its murderous oppressors, and put in force from ocean to ocean and from the Arctic Seas to the Gulf of Mexico the ferocious régime of Loyola and Torquemada, we looked with indifference on its acquisition everywhere of property of immense value, free from taxation, on its creation here of Princes of the Church, on its energetic proselytism, and on its stealthy approaches to power.

There has never been, in this country, any opposition on the part of Freemasonry to Catholicism as a religion. One great and cardinal principle of our Order benig Toleration, perfect and absolute, the right of every man to worship God in accordance with the convictions of his own conscience, we have not even felt indignation when the educational establishments of Catholicism have made priests of our sons, and devotees or nuns of our daughters. With a hundred thousand members of the Roman Catholic faith in its Lodges, in the various Latin countries of the world, the Ancient and Accepted Scottish Rite could have no dislike to Catholicism as a religion. It has only denied its right to compel men to profess a belief in what it might, in its pretended infallibility, decree to be religious truth, and to persecute with rack and fagot, or otherwise, and grill and roast alive those who do not consent to believe that which they cannot believe.

Freemasonry here has not been willing to think that the Head of the oldest and greatest Christian Churches, successor of the penniless Galilean Fisherman Peter, dreamed of renewing and reviving against the Order throughout the whole world, the Bulls of his predecessors Clement and Benedict, and of excommunicating and declaring subject to the heavier penalties of the Church the Emperor and Crown Prince of Germany, Masons and Patrons of Masonry; the Crown Princes of the Netherlands, of Denmark and of Great Britain, and the King of Sweden and Norway, Grand Masters of Masons; the Emperor of Brazil, member of the Supreme Council of that Empire; the President and ex-President of Mexico, the ex-President of Honduras, the President of Venezuela, Sagasta, Prime Minister, and ex-Grand Commander of the Supreme Council of Spain, with hundreds upon hundreds of the great wise men of the age in every civilized country in the world. For, by thus reviving and confirming *all* the enactments of his predecessors, it is decreed that the Inquisition, if its existence and power can be restored, will have the power and right, and find it to be its duty, to cause to be dug up and burned in an *Auto da Fe* (as it has in its days of power and irresponsibility done by its sentences with the mortal remains of relapsed Jews and heretics), the bones of Bishops of the Episcopal Church, of Chief Magistrates of Republics, of great Princes and immortal Patriots, of Riego and Juarez, of Garfield and Garibaldi and Washington.

But suddenly the ghastly spectre of a hideous and frightful Past stands in the twilight after the red sunset of the Papacy, upon the summit of the Vatican, and cries out this baleful proclamation to a startled world:

"For this reason, when We first came to the helm of the Church, We saw and plainly felt that, so far as was possible, We ought to resist this enormous evil by the opposition of our authority. Having often obtained a favourable opportunity, We have attacked the chief heads of the doctrines into which the perversity of Masonic opinions seemed especially to have entered. . . . . Moreover, by the Letter beginning 'Diu-turnum,' we have marked out and set forth *a form of political power in accordance with the principles of Christian wisdom, wonderfully coherent both with the nature of things, and with the safety of Peoples and Princes*. Now, therefore, by the example of our predecessors we have decided to proceed directly against the Masonic Society itself, against their whole teaching, their plans and habit of thought and act, so that the poisonous strength of that Sect may be more and more brought to light, and that this may avail to check the contagion of the dangerous plague."

Thus this letter, beginning *"Humanum Genus," The Human Race*, is not only an open declaration against Free-masonry, unexpected, but not unwelcome; but it is, as will be more fully seen as we proceed further with it, much more than that, and fitly beginning with those words; because, if what has come to pass during the last hundred years, not only in Protestant countries, but in Catholic countries as well, in the matter of civil polity, the advancement of scientific knowledge, and immunity from persecution and torture, has been for the benefit of the Common People, THIS ENCYCLICAL LETTER IS A DECLARATION OF WAR AGAINST THE HUMAN RACE.

It is not unwelcome to Freemasonry, we repeat; not because Freemasonry *desires* hostile relations with the Church of Rome, but because it prefers open war to covert hostility; and it has long known that, in these United States, and especially in Louisiana, the influences of that Church has been constantly exerted against itself, while there has been seeming peace, by attempts to procure renunciation of Masonry from Masons on their deathbeds, and by making wives agents of the Priesthood, to persuade their husbands, if by persuasion they could effect it, and if not, then by persistent discontent and querulous com-plaining, making home a Purgatory, to force them either to renounce Freemasonry altogether or at least to cease to attend the meetings of the Lodges, and be no longer actively engaged in the good works of the Order.

Having informed those to whom the Letter is addressed that he had already expressed to them his views in regard to the proper form and nature of political government, the *Pontifex Maximus* proceeds to allege that Freemasonry is endeavoring to carry into real effect the views of the Materialists; than which nothing could be more untrue, in regard to the Free-masonry of all English-speaking countries; and in reply to which, as to other countries than these, it is true to say that not one Freemason in a thousand anywhere is a Materialist, except in France and Belgium; and that even in these two countries those who are far from being Materialists outnumber the latter five-hundred fold.

The Letter proceeds to make proof of its assertion in these words, speaking of Freemasonry:

"In truth, with long and pertinacious labour, it exerts itself for this purpose, that the rule of the Church should be of no weight, that its authority should be as nothing in a State; *and for this reason they everywhere assert and insist that sacred and civil matters ought to be wholly distinct.* By this they exclude the most wholesome virtue of the Catholic religion *from the laws and from the administration of a country; and the consequence is that they think whole States ought to be constituted outside of the institutes and precepts of the Church."*

In other words, the Roman Church protests against that fundamental principle of constitutional government, dear above almost all else to the people of the United States, that Church and State should act each within its proper sphere, and that with the civil government and political administration of affairs the Church should have nothing to do. The people of the United States do not propose to argue that with the Church of Rome.

"Nor are they content," the letter continues, "with neglecting the Church, their best guide, unless they can injure her by hostility. And, in truth, they are allowed with impunity to attack the very foundations of the Catholic religion by speaking, writing and teaching." Alas! Humanity has at last an opportunity, not in Protestant countries only, but in Italy itself, in Spain and Portugal, in Mexico and Brazil, and all South America, in speech and writing, to utter its thoughts, arraign its oppressors and defend the rights given it by God; and there is no longer an Inquisition to burn at the stake those who are too free with tongue or pen. The people of the United States will never permit any Church to circumscribe the freedom of the press; nor can they ever be made to believe that free discussion will be for the discomfiture of Truth and to the profit of Error, unless God ceases to be on the side of the Truth.

The Letter then complains of various measures of the Italian Government to the injury of the Papacy; as to which that government is probably not afraid of the Pope's appeal to the public opinions of the world. One sentence only we quote: "We see the Societies of religious Orders overturned and dispersed." Yes, on the 3rd of September, 1759, all Jesuits were banished from Portugal and its dominions; and other Catholic countries, not urged thereto by Freemasonry, have found it necessary to their own peace and well-being to do the same. And it proved to be an unfortunate day for Brazil when, not very many years ago, offering an asylum to the Jesuits expelled from other countries, it entrusted to them the charge of the public institutions of education; and Jesuitism and Ultramontanism undertook to possess themselves of the government of the country and suppress Freemasonry.

"If," the Pope says, "those who are enrolled into their number are by no means ordered to forswear in set form the Catholic Institutions, this indeed is so far from being repugnant to the designs of Freemasons that it rather serves them. For, in the first place, they easily deceive in this way the simple **and incautious,** and offer attractions to far more persons. *Then, moreover, by accepting any that present themselves, no matter of what religion, they gain their purpose of urging* THAT GREAT ERROR OF THE PRESENT DAY, *viz., that questions of religion ought to be left undetermined, and that there should be no distinction made between varieties.* AND THIS POLICY AIMS AT THE DESTRUCTION OF ALL RELIGIONS, ESPECIALLY AT THAT OF THE CATHOLIC RELIGION, WHICH, SINCE IT IS THE ONLY TRUE ONE, CANNOT BE REDUCED TO EQUALITY WITH THE REST WITHOUT THE GREATEST INJURY."

Questions of religion, then, must not be left undetermined, and distinction must be made between varieties; and the Catholic religion must be determined to be the only true one. How? By what power? By the Sovereign, by the Civil Power, or shall the power to decree itself the only Church "possessed of the Kingdom of God," be admitted to be inherent in the Catholic Church itself? Of course, this. Is not the Pope infallible? Is he not Jove, and *Divus, and Iste Deus?* In either case, the power to prohibit the existence of all other Churches must follow; the power to punish adherence to other creeds as heresies, civil power and criminal jurisdiction, the power of repression, of punishing relapses, must be vested in the Jesuits, and in the Inquisition, revived, and armed with all its old powers. All means to effect the absolutely necessary end of suppression and extirpation must be legitimate, and the reign of the Devil of persecution and torture must begin again.

Freemasonry opens its doors to men of all religions alike; and the most splendid jewel of the prerogative of the Scottish Freemasonry in the Southern Jurisdiction of the United States is, that on Maundy Thursday and Easter Sunday the Episcopal clergyman and Hebrew rabbi can and do stand together at its altars, in presence of the Seven Lights, the latter thanking God that he has at length found one place where he is the perfect equal and full brother of men of the Christian faith. Never, never will *that* Freemasonry permit this jewel to be filched from it by craft and treachery and fraud and falsehood, or torn from it by force. It has been once attempted here and failed; and it will always fail.

The Encyclical Letter then makes this extraordinary statement, to which every Freemason in every English-speaking country in the world, and those of every other, with but two or three exceptions, will oppose either an indignant or contemptuous denial; for, as a charge against Freemasonry in general, it is a shameless libel:

"But, in truth, the Sect *grants great license to its initiates,* allowing them to defend either position, that there is a God, or that there is no God; *and those who resolutely maintain that there is none are initiated as easily as those who think indeed that there is a God, but hold about him views as depraved as are those of the Pantheists."*

The Grand Orient of France has been proclaimed by the Freemasonry of Great Britain and the United States to be no longer a Masonic power, because it has struck out of its Constitution the requirement of a declaration of belief in the existence of a God; not denying it, but, as it claims, leaving entire freedom of conscience.   And when the Convention of certain Supreme Councils at Lausanne substituted for the word "God" the phrases *"Force Supérieure"* and *"Principe Créative,"* we denounced it as a departure from Masonic principles, and it was finally abandoned.   By the Ancient Ritual of Freemasonry and by its fundamental Law, no Atheist can be made a Mason, any more than a woman can; and no person can be initiated without kneeling "for the benefit of Lodge prayer" and professing that he puts his trust in God.   It is true that there are Lodges in France and Belgium, and perhaps in Italy, which do not deny initiation to one professing himself an Atheist; but these are condemned with almost entire unanimity everywhere else in the world.   Freemasonry is not responsible for private vagaries of unbelief in France.   If its principles were what the Pope alleges them to be, there would not be thousands of clergymen, Episcopalians, Presbyterians, and of other denominations, members of Masonic Lodges in all the English-speaking countries, and very many of them members of the higher Bodies of the Ancient and Accepted Scottish Rite.

The Pope next proceeds to speak of the subjects of marriage, education and civil government; and it is herein that the full scope and intent of the Letter appear.

The Materialists, he says, have this system: "Marriage, they say, belongs to the class of contracts; it can lawfully be rescinded at the will of the contracting parties; and power as regards the marriage tie is in the hands of the civil rulers.   In educating children, they consider that no religious instruction should be given according to any fixed and determined purpose;

it is to be open to each, when grown up, to follow what religion he may prefer."

And then he says: "*Freemasons, moreover, clearly assent to these very principles; and not only do they assent, but they are, and have long been, anxious to introduce them into habit and usage.*"

To prove this, for it is the only thing that he offers in justification of the assertion, he says: "Already in many regions, and those, too, belonging to the Catholic faith, it is decided that no marriages shall be deemed lawful except those contracted by the civil rite; in some places divorces are allowed by law; in other places efforts are being made that they should be so allowed as soon as possible. *Thus, what they are hastening to is,* that the nature of marriage may be converted into unstable and temporary unions, which passion may form, and passion again dissolve."

Pope Leo XIII. does not know, and has not a shred of evidence to convince him, that Freemasonry takes into consideration, *in any way,* the question of the mode of marriage. That is a matter wholly foreign to Freemasonary, and about which as an Order it has never sought to ascertain the collective opinion of members. Each has his own opinion, whatever it may be; and no other Mason has anything to do with that opinion. Marriage has been declared by legislation in many countries to be a civil contract; but it is certainly not known among Masons that Freemasonry, as an Order, or by any sort of concert among any considerable number of its members, has borne any part in procuring such legislation anywhere. We doubt if any Masons in England or the United States ever heard the subject mentioned in a Lodge. Nothing could more certainly tend to dissension; for very many Freemasons everywhere agree to a great extent with the Church of Rome in its views of marriage and divorce. Of these I am one.

Again, the Pope quite recklessly says: "However, with the utmost harmony of intentions, the Sect of Freemasons has this also in view—*to seize for itself the education of youth.*" Their object, he says, is to mould those of tender age, and pervert them to their own ends. "Wherefore, in the education and teaching of boys, they allow the Ministers of the Church no share in direction or watchfulness; and already in several places *they have gained their point,* that the whole training of youth should be in the hands of the Laity; *and that also in forming their characters there should be no mixture of those great and most holy duties which unite man to God.*"

Freemasonry has turned its attention to the education of the young, so far only as it has here and there established institutions of very moderate pretensions, for the education of children of poor or deceased Brethren of the Order. It is quite true that it has not seen fit to entrust such schools to the care and charge of the Roman Catholic Clergy, its enemies; but the offices of religion are in none of them disregarded. The Order has never made any attempt anywhere "to seize for itself the education of youth." It has never endeavored anywhere "to gain the point that the whole training of youths should be in the hands of the Laity." It has meddled with that matter just as little as it has meddled with the subject of marriage; and there are as many different opinions among Freemasons upon the one subject as upon the other; but what these opinions are Freemasonry does not inquire. It has not been the Freemasons who have settled these things in the United States. Each of them has acted on his own private opinion in regard to each without any Masonic organization or concert of action whatever.

But Pope Leo XIII. desired to denounce the laws which in many countries make marriage a civil contract and allow divorces, and the laws, institutions, corporations, and associations which maintain schools, academies and colleges unconnected with the churches; and especially, perhaps, those laws which do not permit any portion of the monies raised by public taxation or appropriated by our States for the support of public schools to be placed in the hands of the Roman Catholic Clergy for the maintenance of schools to be managed by them, and in which children are to be educated to become Roman Catholics.

And this portion of his Letter, so entirely foreign to the subject of Freemasonry, is evidently a mandate of urgency to the Catholic Clergy and Laity to secure active, combined and persistent effort by them hereafter, *in the United States*, and elsewhere, to have marriage made no longer a civil contract, but a Sacrament of Holy Church, with prohibition of divorce; and to obtain for the Catholic Clergy the control, as far as it can be done, of the public education of the young, and of a share of the funds furnished for that purpose by the public.

If the Jesuits and other clergy who manage and conduct the Catholic Schools and Seminaries in the United States are also instructed by it to devote their efforts hereafter to converting to Caltholicism the children of Protestants who may be entrusted to them for tuition, so that each school and seminary and college is to be an institution *de Propaganda fide*, it will be manly and honest to avow this openly. The suppressions of the true and suggestions of the false, once justified by the Disciples of Loyola and exposed by Pascal, are not now regarded by honest men as consistent with religious duty or personal honour or common honesty. Hitherto, though many converts to

Catholicism, especially among pupils of that sex which is more sensitive to religious influences than the other, have returned to their homes from Roman Catholic Seminaries, the managers of these have always protested that all attempts to convert pupils were scrupulously refrained from; and these protestations have been believed; many Protestants, indeed, not being unwilling that their children, if fairly dealt with, should embrace the Roman Catholic faith, if their convictions should lead them to do so. Unquestionably the Encyclical Letter contains a vigorous denunciation of the omission of the special religious instruction of that Church in the education of the young, and chides all who neglect the work of proselyting.

The letter then proceeds to state the materialistic "principles of statesmanship." It says: "They maintain *that all things are vested in a free people; that power is held by the order or permission of that people, so that, if the popular pleasure change, Princes may be degraded from their rank even against their will.* They assert *that the source of all laws and civil duties is either in the multitude, or in the power that rules the State, and this when formed by the newest teaching.*" And the Letter avers "that these very sentiments are equally pleasing to the Freemasons; and that they wish to arrange States after this likeness and pattern, is too well known to need demonstration. For long indeed they have been openly working for this object with all their strength and resources."

These are the political principles of all English-speaking Masons; not because they are Freemasons, not because these principles are taught in their lodges, for they teach nothing there in regard to politics or systems of government; but because they are Englishmen, Scotsmen, Irishmen, or citizens of the United States, and their civil governments are founded upon these principles. In other countries these are the principles which have always inspired the Ancient and Acceptd Scottish Rite and the French or Modern Rite; and these Rites have therefore always been the advocates and champions, especially in the Latin countries of Europe, of freedom and constitutional government; and in this chiefly consist their glory and their honour. The Roman Catholic Church has been always and everywhere on the side of the arbitrary power of Princes and Potentates; Masonry on the side of the people. Thou hast said truly, O Pope!

Then the Successor of Saint Peter thus announces to the Faithful the law by which they are to be absolutely governed—the law of the Divine right of anointed Princes:

"As men are born by the will of God for civil union and association, and as the power of ruling is so necessary a bond of civil society, that on its removal that society must suddenly be severed, *it follows that He who gave birth to society gives birth also to the rule of authority.* WHENCE IT IS UNDERSTOOD THAT HE IN WHOM POWER IS, WHOEVER HE IS, IS GOD'S MINISTER. Wherefore, so far as the end and nature of human society require, it is as right to obey lawful authority, when it issues just orders, *as it is to obey the power of God who rules all things; and this is pre-eminently inconsistent with truth,* THAT IT SHOULD DEPEND UPON THE WILL OF THE PEOPLE TO CAST OFF OBEDIENCE AT ITS PLEASURE."

Is every one, then, who finds himself *actually* possessing power, *thereby* God's Minister? Was Cromwell God's Minister? Was William of Orange God's Minister? Was Napoleon the Great? Were William and Mary God's Ministers? Are the King and Parliament of Italy God's Ministers? Are the Emperors of Germany and Brazil God's Ministers? Oh, no! The Pope means those in whom power is, they having *lawful* authority, *i. e., those whose rule and power are sanctioned by the Church.* How, according to his doctrine, if it be pre-eminently inconsistent with truth" that the *people* may rid a country of a ferocious and brutal tyrant by compelling his abdication—of a Ferdinand VII., or Philip II. (whose will and that of the Church of Rome Alva executed in the Netherlands, leaving written there all over the land the never-to-be-effaced records of the blood-guiltiness of the Church and King)—of a Bomba, of a Nero, of a Caligula, of a Borgia—how is any bloody and brutal miscreant, wearing the purple, to be dethroned? Must the people endure until God shall remove the butchering malefactor by death, that perhaps Commodus may succeed Tiberius, or a worse and meaner tyrant follow Bomba?

There must be *some* power on earth to set free a suffering people. It must not "depend upon the will of the people to cast off obedience *at its pleasure*—all Catholics are ordered to believe." When, then? When THE CHURCH may authorize it; when the Pope may declare the Throne forfeited for crime, and excommunicate the Ruler, as Heretic or Freemanson? Is it not this that is meant?

Thus the Pope pronounces by his prerogative of infallibility, and as Vicegerent of God, whom it is as unlawful to refuse to obey as it is to refuse "to obey the power of God, who rules all things," that the dethronement of James II., Catholic King of England, was an act of disobedience of the power of God.

"On the contempt for the authority of Princes, on the allowing and approving of lust for sedition, on the granting of full license to the passions of the people, bridled only by the fear of punishment, there must of necessity arise a change and overthrow of all things."

The Freemasons, he passionately cries, "have begun to have great weight in ruling States, but they are ready to shake the foundations of Empires, and to censure, accuse and drive out the chief men of a State, whenever its administration seems different from their wishes. Just so have they deluded the people by their flattery. By calling in sounding terms for liberty and public prosperity, and saying that it is owing to the Church and Princes that the people are not delivered from unjust slavery and want, they have imposed upon the populace, and have instigated it by a thirst for revolution to attack the power of both."

Where? Garibaldi, in Italy, was a Freemason, and there are perhaps a hundred and fifty Masonic lodges in Italy; and yet a King rules peacefully there, upheld by the Freemasons, his Minister, Depretis, being a Mason. In Brazil the Emperor is a Freemason of the 33d Degree, and there have been no insurrections or disturbances of the public peace there, though the Freemasons assemble in some two hundred Lodges and higher Bodies. In Portugal there are a Grand Orient and Supreme Council and sixty or seventy Lodges, and the Marshal Duke Saldanha, who by peaceful revolution gave that Kingdom a constitutional government, was ex-Grand Master of Masons; and yet a King reigns peacefully in Portugal. In Spain there are two hundred Lodges, and Sagasta is a Freemason, and Alfonso reigns secure, his throne upheld by Freemasonry.

Attacks upon the Church and Princes, the Pope exclaims, instigated by Freemasons, have given the people greater expectation than reality of advantage. "Nay, rather, the common people, suffering worse oppression, are for the most part forced to be without those very alleviations of their miseries, which they would find with ease and abundance, *if matters were arranged according to Christian ordinances*. But as many as strive AGAINST THE ORDER ARRANGED BY DIVINE PROVIDENCE usually pay this penalty for their pride, that they meet with a wretched and miserable fortune in the quarter whence they rashly expected prosperity and success."

The Spanish colonies in the New World threw off by revolt the intolerable yoke of oppression of the Spanish Crown, and made themselves free Republics. They were not content with "matters arranged according to Christian Ordinances" by the Catholic Church, for the benefit of a rapacious and cruel government, with those "Ordinances" administered by Inquisitors. Are the people of Mexico losers thereby? Are those of Chilé or Venezuela? The Netherlands, bled nearly unto death, at last, by heroic endurance and matchless courage, rescued their country from the Satanic rule of Alva. France put an end to such Saturnalia of Hell there as that of the Eve of St. Bartholomew, and in carrying away the Pope to Avignon paid Rome in full for the blood with which the grey hairs of old Coligni dabbled the stones of Paris. God, by the instrumentality of

Luther, avenged the murder of Albigenses and Lollards, Huss and Wiclif, Jerome of Prague and Savonarola, seriously disarranging "matters arranged according to Christian Ordinances." Has all this been to the manifest disavantage of the people of the liberated countries of the world? Have the Netherlands, Belgium, Portugal, Italy, lost by it? Is France miserable and suffering? Is Germany wretched? Does Great Britain languish for want of the tender mercies of the Papacy?

That great statesman, Edmund Burke, said that he did not know how to draw an indictment against a whole people; but we have thus shown, by the very words, faithfully translated, of the Roman Pontiff himself, that this Encyclical Letter, which purports to be only an arraignment and condemnation of Freemasonry, is in its principle intent and deepest significance and indictment, not only of the people of every Republic and Constitutional Monarchy in the world, but of every Protestant country in the world; and not only of the people of every Protestant country in the world, but of all that portion of the people of every Catholic country who have in these later centuries asserted the right of the people to have a voice in the affairs of government, and to be secure in their persons and lives against the infernal methods of procedure, the creation of imaginary crimes, and the cruel torturings upon mere suspicion, of such tribunals as the Inquisition. It is a sentence purporting to be uttered by the voice of God, outlawing and excluding from Heaven all the patriots and lovers of liberty and liberators of the people, all the array of martyrs who have died in endeavoring to vindicate the right of humanity to freedom of thought and conscience.

It denounces as wicked and criminal, and contrary to the ordinances of the Christian religion, not only the laws which permit the solemnization of marriage by the civil magistrate, and those which exclude sectarian religious teachings from schools and seminaries maintained by public taxation; not only the constitutional provisions which in all the States of these United States decree the separation of Church and State, and refuse to the Church any part in the civil government of the country; not only those by which the pretensions of the Churches and their right to dictate opinions may be freely discussed by the public press; but also the great principle on which the governments of all Republics are founded, of the sovereignty of the people, the only legitimate source and author of civil power and government. It asserts the divine right of Princes, *if held by the Church of Rome to have lawful authority,* to govern men against their will; that they are the Ministers of God; and that the people have no power to free themselves from the tyranny and oppression of these divinely commissioned scourges and Assassins of Humanity.

It is an indictment of Humanity itself, for its instinctive struggles to lift itself above the miseries and indignities of bodily and intellectual bondage to Priest and Potentate; for the involuntary and irrepressible aspirations of its soul towards light and knowledge and the free atmosphere of intellectual expansion; and for the not more involuntary quiverings of its tortured, racked, wrenched and mutilated muscles and nerves. It is an indictment of Civilization, of Progress, of the Spirit of Manhood, of the self-respect of the Peoples, of the Progress onward and upward of Humanity, of the Spirit of the Age, which is the very Inspiration of God; and of God Himself and the beneficient Provinces of God, who loves the people in rags, hungry and hopeless, better than He loves the Priests in scarlet and the Tyrants in purple.

In renewing and by his Apostolic authority confirming everything decreed by former Popes against Freemasonry, ratifying their Bulls as well in general as in particular, Leo XIII. leaves to his faithful subjects no discretionary power to regard any portions of those anathemas as obsolete, or to pay respect and obedience to those laws, Bills of Right, or Constitutions of the countries in which they live, which may forbid the enforcement of the commands of the Church contained in these Bulls.

For he immediately adds: "Having entire confidence in this respect, in the good will of those who are Christians, we beseech them, in the name of their eternal salvation, and WE DEMAND of them *to make it for themselves a sacred obligation of conscience,* NEVER TO DEPART, EVEN BY ONE SINGLE LINE, FROM THE MANDATES PROMULGATED ON THIS SUBJECT BY THE APOSTOLIC SEE."

He then poceeds to direct by what measures and devices the Clergy are "to cause to disappear the impure contagion of the poison which circulates in the veins of society, and infects it throughout."

First—By tearing off the mask of Freemasonry, and showing it as it is.

Second—By special discourses and pastoral letters to instruct the people. "Remind the people," he says, that by virtue of the decrees often issued by our predecessors, no Catholic, if he desires to continue worthy of the name, and to have for his salvation the concern which it deserves, can, under any pretext, affiliate with the Sect of Freemasons."

Then, by frequent instructions and exhortations to help the masses to acquire a knowledge of religion, expounding, in writing and orally, the elements of the sacred principles which constitute the Christian philosophy; and so to increase the devotion of Clergy and Laity to the Catholic Church, the result whereof will be increased disgust for secret societies and greater care to avoid them. To which method of inculcating what is believed by the Church to be truth, and opposing the progress of what it believes to be error, a Freemason will be the last man in the world to object, if it is not to be supplemented by other too well-known methods.

And, to engage with great zeal in increasing and strengthening the Third Order of Saint Francis, in the discipline whereof the Pope claims to have made wise modifications, so that "it may be able to render great service in helping to overcome *the contagion of these detestable Sects."*

Third—To re-engage in establishing corporations of workingmen to protect, under the tutorship of religion, the interests of labor and the morals of workers; with societies of patrons, to assist and instruct the prolétaires, such as is the Society of Saint Vincent de Paul.

Fourth—Vigilantly to watch with pastoral solicitude over the young, drawing them away, by renewed efforts, from the schools and teachers where they would be exposed to breathe the poisoned breath of the Sects; parents, teachers and curates, urged by the Bishops, guarding their children and pupils against "these criminal societies," which are ever endeavoring to ensnare them; those who have it in charge to prepare young persons to receive the sacraments, inducing every one of them to take a firm resolution not to join any society without the knowledge of their parents or without having consulted their curate or confessor.

For the rest, to implore the aid of the Lord, with great ardor and reiterated solicitations, proportioned to the necessity of the circumstances and the intensity of the peril.

Haughty on account of its former successes, the Sect of Freemasons insolently erects its head, and its audacity no longer seems to know any bounds. United to one another by the bond of a criminal federation, and by their secret plans, its adepts lend to each other mutual support and incite each other to dare and to do evil."

"To which violent attack an energetic defense must respond. Good men must unite and form an immense coalition of prayers and efforts. Especially the Virgin Mary, Mother of God, must be besought to become the auxiliary and interpreter of the Church, displaying her power against the Sects which are reviving the rebellious spirit, the incorrigible perfidy, and the cunning of the Devil. Saint Michael, who precipitated the revolted angels into hell; Saint Joseph, husband of the Virgin, and the great Apostles Saint Peter and Saint Paul, must also be enlisted; and thus the imminent danger to the human race may be averted."

Instruction of the people in religious doctrine; enlargement of the Third Order of Franciscans, organization of associations of workingmen; gaining control of the education of the young, and incessant prayer—these are to be the ostensible means of offense and defense. *A la bonne heure!* if no more were meant. But the Church of Rome has never been in the habit of making known the real means or instruments which it has determined to use for the suppression of heresy or to repress the struggles of Humanity to escape from the intolerable burdens of oppression; and it is not likely to do it now. The ostentatious recital of these peaceful means of antagonism does not agree with the explicit re-enactments of the Bulls of Clement and Benedict. The Church has other measures in view than teaching and prayer; and it is already using them in Belgium and Brazil. It has mysteries the divulgation of which is interdicted; Conclaves and Consistories, Generals of the Order, Assemblies that are secret, as their decisions and the means and agents of execution are. The adepts blindly and without discussion obey the injunctions of their chiefs, holding themselves always ready, upon the slightest notification or hardly perceptible sign, to execute the orders given them, devoting themselves in advance, in case of disobedience, to the most terrible penalties, and even to death, were the order even to bring about the murder of another William the Silent or of the Chiefs of a Republic.

With such a Past as that of the Church of Rome is, it would have been wise not to provoke comment upon its real crimes by accusing others of having committed imaginary ones; or exposure of the doctrines of the Jesuits by libeling those of Freemasonry.

It is not only just and fair and reasonable, but of absolute necessity, to conclude that anyone who speaks to men by authority *intends* the consequences that may naturally, anywhere, be the effects of his words. It is even of absolute necessity, sometimes, to conclude that ambiguous phrases and significant suggestions and veiled meanings, when used as they are here, are employed to induce the commission of infamies, the explicit incitation whereunto might startle the conscience of Humanity. And this is especially of unavoidable necessity, in the interpretation of the mandates of the Church of Rome, against those whom it considers its enemies. For it has never yet repudiated and condemned the maxims of the Spanish Jesuits or declared the suppression of the Truth or the suggestion of Falsehood, for the benefit of the Church, to be contrary to the Spirit of the Gospel, or confessed itself ashamed for having so long employed the infernal enginery of the Inquisition. It is infallible, can never have erred, can never change. It long ago lost all right to expect the world to give it credit for honesty of intention or frankness of expression.

This new Proclamation of Interdict and Excommunication is, it is probable, more especially intended as a political manifesto to the Clergy and Catholics of Italy, Spain, Portugal, Belgium and Brazil, inciting them to treasonable plottings and combinations against the Constitutional Governments of those countries. It preaches to them a new Crusade, the purpose whereof is to destroy those governments, to depose the Monarchs who permit the existence of Freemasonry in their dominions and the expression of the voice of the people in public affairs; and to place in those Kingdoms the education of the young in the hands of the soldiery of Loyola, and the power of persecuting Freemasonry and Heresy and the favouring of liberal government in the Holy Office or Inquisition, armed with all its old inhuman and unchristian powers, against which the sense of justice of the whole world long ago revolted. In Brazil it incites the Archbishop of Rio de Janeiro and the Bishop of Pará, and all the Jesuits and Ultramontane Clergy, to renew the war a few years ago waged by them against Freemasonry, against the Emperor and Parliament, and the Laws of the Empire, acting towards the Emperor as towards one excommunicated, reprobated and accursed.

Thus it menaces the public peace in those countries, inciting revolt and insurrection and assassination, and makes the Lord's Prayer the patent of an Inquisitor, and the Sermon on the Mount a warrant for murder.

Already the General of the Jesuits and the Chief Inquisitor of the Holy Office have promulgated their orders to their troops and officials, commanding them to use their utmost exertions to carry into effect the mandates of the Encyclical Letter. In Spain and Portugal secret anti-Masonic associations are already being organized under these orders, and like organizations may be looked for in the United States, with resort to every other means of warfare against the great principles which Freemasonry represents, that can be *prudently* and *safely* employed.

It is also a political manifesto, and more, for our neighboring Republic of Mexico, and those of Central and South America. There are Grand Lodges and Supreme Councils of Masons in most of them; and in all Masonry is free to exist and work undisturbed, and is powerful and influential. In Mexico the ex-President, now President-elect, of the Republic, and the Actual President are 33ds, members of the Supreme Council of Mexico created by us, as the President Comonfort was a 33d, Grand Commander of that Supreme Council, and as the President Juarez was a Mason. It is well known that the population at large of the Republic is uneducated and grossly ignorant, and slavishly subservient to the Priesthood; and that it detests and hates Protestants as heretics, damned by the anathemas of the Church, and unfit to live. The Priesthood in Mexico has always been the uncompromising and wily enemy of every patriotic President, of Republican Government, of Freemasonry, of the principles on which constitutional governments are founded, and of all the men by whose sublime efforts and sacrifices Mexico was made and has been maintained a Republic.

It is also well known that, in consequence of the friendly relations between our two Republics, and the extension of railroads in Mexico, built by the capital of our citizens, there now are in that country a great number of citizens of the United States, many of whom have purchased mines and lands and are working and cultivating them. The Letter HUMANUM GENUS is so framed and worded as to be calculated, and must therefore be taken to be artfully and deliberately intended to incite the Priesthood in Mexico to renewed zeal against heresy and heretics, and more persistent and continuous and better organized and more audacious efforts to destroy Freemasonry there, and overturn Republicanism. If citizens of the United States peaceably engaged there in useful avocations should be assassinated by mobs, instigated, if not openly led, by the Priests; if Diaz and Gonzales and other Freemasons should be murdered and the Church should inaugurate a bloody civil war, Pope Leo XIII. will not be able, by any special pleading, to avoid the responsibility for all the fatal consequences that may ensue

For men have not forgotten that Ignatus Loyola, founder of the Order of Jesus, promulgated this law.

"Visum est nobis in Domino nullas Constitutiones posse obligationem ad peccatum *mortale* vel veniale inducere, *nisi Superior* (in nomine J.-C. vel in virtute obedientiæ), *juberet.*"

"It has seemed to us in the Lord that no Constitutions can make it obligatory to commit a mortal or a pardonable sin *unless the Superior* (in the name of Jesus Christ, or in virtue of obedience) *may so order.*"

No doubt the General of the Jesuits holds the same doctrine today, and is ready to apply it, if occasion should demand, *that the Superior in the Order has the power to command an inferior to commit a mortal sin.* It is a *fruitful* and *convenient* doctrine, when the matter in hand is to destroy Constitutional Governments in Catholic countries.

There is still more to be considered by the people of the United States; which, when they come fully to comprehend the purport of this manifesto from the Vatican, they *will* consider. The Catholics, whom it proposes to organize into Italian colonies or camps here, obeying the laws enacted at Rome, regulating their political action by principles hostile to those on which Republican Government is founded, and sedulously inculcating these upon the young entrusted to their charge, are being thoroughly informed of its contents and meaning; for it is already being read in all their churches. Those whose principles it damns as detestable and wicked will come to the knowledge of it more slowly, feeling, even if Freemasons, little interest in a Papal Bull against Freemasonry, and little inclined to read so long a paper; and slow to believe that it is an attack upon the civil institutions and system of government under which they live. But they will well understand it by and by and have something to say in regard to it.

It makes it to be of divine obligation for every faithful Catholic in the United States *to be at heart the mortal and uncompromising enemy of the principles and spirit, the plan and purpose, of the Government under which he lives, and whose equal laws permit him to plot and conspire against it with impunity.* It proclaims it to the devout believer as a truth spoken by the mouth of God, that the great axiomatic principles, dear to the lovers of human liberty in every age, dear especially, dear beyond price or expression, to the people of the United States, on which, as upon the immovable adamant of eternal Truth, their systems of government is builded, are *false* and *criminal* and *wicked*, making the United States to be a part of the Kingdom of Satan.

It makes it his and her duty, therefore, to do all that it may be possible to do to eradicate these principles and destroy all that is builded upon them; to gain control, so far as possible, of the education of youth and convert the young to the Catholic faith; to win or buy for the Catholic Church a power and influence in the government of the country

Already the Encyclical Letter is acted upon as a political manifesto in Ireland.

Archbishop McCabe, we are told, has written a letter with reference to the approaching election of Lord Mayor for Dublin. He says he is unable to understand how Catholics could in honor and conscience cast their votes for Mr. Winstanley, who is both a Home Ruler and a Freemason. "As a Freemason he is a member of a society which aims to overthrow religion. To Freemasonry the revolutions of the last century were traceable. No one can plead non-participation as long as he remains a Mason."

And Mr. Winstanley has repudiated Freemasonry to obtain votes; and he has been defeated.

But—for which thanks be unto the God of Hosts, "from whom all glories are!"—Freemasonry is mightier than the Church of Rome; for it possesses the invincible might of the Spirit of the Age and of the convictions of civilized Humanity; and it will continue to grow in strength and greatness, while that Church in love with and doting upon its old traditions, and incapable of learning anything, will continue to decay. The palsied hand of the Papacy is too feeble to arrest the march of human progress. It cannot bring back the obsolete doctrine that Kings reign by divine right. In vain it will preach new Crusades against Freemasonry, or Heresy, or Republicanism. It will continue to sigh in vain for the return of the days of Philip II. and Mary of England, of Loyola and Alva and Torquemada. If it succeeds in instigating the Kings of Spain and Portugal to engage in the work of extirpating Freemasonry, these will owe it to the speedy loss of their crowns. The world is no longer in a humour to be saddled and bitted like an ass and ridden by Capuchins and Franciscans. Humanity has inhaled the fresh, keen winds of freedom, and has escaped from companionship with the herds that chew the cud and the inmates of stables and kennels, to the highlands of Liberty, Equality and Brotherhood.

The world is not likely to forget that the infallible Pope Urban VIII., Barberini, set his signature to the sentence which condemned to perpetual imprisonment, to adjuration and to silence, Galileo Galilei, who, it is known, avoided being burned at the stake by denying on bended knees the deductions of positive science, which demonstrated the movement of the earth; and on the 2d day of July, 1633, the Cardinal of Santo Onofio Barberini, in the name of the Pope his uncle, announced to the world the condemnation of Galileo by an Encyclical Letter, from the Latin whereof we translate these words: *"For which matter Galileo, accused and confined in the prisons of the Holy Office, has been condemned to adjure the said opinion. . . ."*

Nor are Freemasons likely to forget that when the Bull of Clement XII., which Leo XIII. now revives and re-enacts, was published, Cardinal Firrao explained the nature of the punishments which were required to be inflicted on Masons, and what the kind of service was which the Pope demanded from "the Secular Arm."

"It is forbidden," he says . . . "to affiliate one's self with the Societies of Masons . . . UNDER PENALTY OF DEATH AND OF CONFISCATION OF GOODS, AND TO DIE UNABSOLVED, AND WITHOUT HOPE OF SALVATION." Who will be audacious enough to censure us for replying defiantly to a decree which, by revivor of the Bull of Clement, condemns every Freemason in the world to death and confiscation, and damns him in advance to die without hope of salvation?

The world has not forgotten that when Charles IX. of France and the Duc de Guise at first disowned responsibility for the massacre of 20,000 Protestants, and others, on the Eve and after the Eve of St. Bartholomew, the Catholic Clergy assumed it. Heaven adopted it, they said: "it was not the massacre of the King and the Duke; *it was the Justice of God.*" Then the slaughter recommenced, of neighbor by neighbor, of women, of children, of children unborn, in order to extinguish families, the wombs of the mothers cut open, and the children torn from them, for fear they might survive. "The paper would weep if we should write upon it all that was done."

Men remember that at Saint-Michel, the Jesuit Auger, sent thither from the College of Paris, announced to Bordeaux that the Archangel Michael had made the great massacre, and deplored the sluggishness of the Governor and Magistrates of Bordeaux. After the 24th of August there were feasts. The Catholic Clergy had' theirs, at Paris, on the 28th, and ordered a jubilee, to which the King and Court went, and returned thanks to God. And the King, who proclaimed that he had caused Coligni to be killed, and that he would have poniarded him with his own hand, was flattered to intoxication by the praises and congratulations of Rome. Do men not remember that there were feasts and great gaities at Rome on account of the massacre? That the Pope chaunted the Te Deum Laudamus, and sent to "his son," Charles IX. (to win for whom the whole credit of the massacre the Cardinal of Lorraine moved heaven and earth), the Rose of Gold? That a medal was coined by Rome to commemorate it; and that a painting of the bloody scene was made, and until lately hung in the Vatican?

Freemasonry is strong enough everywhere now to defend itself, and does not dread even the Hierarchy of the Roman Church, with its great revenues, and its Cardinal Princes, claiming to issue the Decrees and Bulletins of God, and to hold the keys with which it locks and unlocks at pleasure the Gates of Paradise. The powers of Freemasonry, too, sending their words to one another over the four continents and the great islands of the Southern seas, colonized by Englishmen, speak, but with only the authority of reason, *Urbi et Orbi*, to men of free souls and high courage and quick intelligence.

It does not need that Freemasonry should take up arms of any sort against the Church of Rome. Science, the wider knowledge of what God is, learned from His works; the irresistible progress of Civilization, the Spirit of the Nineteenth Century; these are the sufficient avengers of the mutilations and murders of the long ages of the horrid Past. These have already avenged Humanity, and Freemasonry need not add another word—

Except these—that there are two questions to be asked, and answer thereunto demanded of all Roman Catholics in the United States who are loyal to the Constitution of Government under which they live, patriotic citizens of the United States:

Do not your consciences tell you that what is now demanded of you by Pope Leo XIII., by the General of the Jesuits and Chief Inquisitor is, TO ENGAGE ACTIVELY IN A CONSPIRACY AGAINST THAT CONSTITUTION OF GOVERNMENT, AND THE PRINCIPLES ON WHICH IT IS FOUNDED; AFTER THE DETHRONEMENT OF WHICH PRINCIPLES THAT CONSTITUTION OF GOVERNMENT COULD NOT LIVE AN HOUR?

If you cannot see it in that light, *do not your consciences and common sense tell you that* TO APPROVE AND FAVOUR AND GIVE AID AND ASSISTANCE TO AN OPEN CONSPIRACY AGAINST EVERY OTHER REPUBLIC AND EVERY CONSTITUTIONAL MONARCHY IN THE WORLD, AND THE PRINCIPLES ON WHICH THEY ARE FOUNDED, IS TO PLAY A PART THAT IS INCONSISTENT WITH THE PRINCIPLES THAT YOU PROFESS TO BE GOVERNED BY HERE, IS IN OPPOSITION TO ALL THE SYMPATHIES OF THE COUNTRY IN WHICH YOU LIVE, AND IS HOSTILE TO THE INFLUENCES OF ITS EXAMPLE AMONG THE PEOPLE OF OTHER COUNTRIES, TREACHEROUS TO YOUR OWN COUNTRY, AND UNWORTHY OF AMERICAN CITIZENS?

You will have to answer these questions, for they will not cease to be reiterated until you do, AND NOT BY FREEMASONRY ALONE.

Given at the Grand Orient aforesaid, the first day of August, 1884, and of the Supreme Council the 84th year.

The Grand Commander,

Albert Pike sig   33°.˙.

FROM

"PROFESSION OF FAITH OF THE XIXTH CENTURY,"

BY EUGENE PELLETAN.

6th Edition, 1864.

Part XI.—Chapter I.

LUTHER.

The hour of the Renascence had sounded. A breath of life passed over Europe.

* * * * * * * * *

One would have said that Italy had found again a lost moiety of her genius: she had, as it were, the intoxication of the Renascence: in it she forgot the gloomy doctrine of the Middle Age, the religion of the Christ Crucified, of the God of Penitence, together. The Papacy itself participated in this universal conspiracy of Paganism. Leo X. had just ascended the Throne of Saint Peter: he was a virtuoso Pope, who loved music and literature. Instead of calling around him the bilious Theologians of Minerva, the long-beards of Inquisitors, pale with watchings and fastings, the body-guard, in a word, of the Theocracy, he drew to him all the Pagans of his time, all the Poets of reflection, and the Dilettanti of the Virgilian diction or of the Ciceronian period, of the music even more than of the thought, of antiquity.

To some he gave a prebend, to others an abbey; to those a bishopric, to these the red cap of a cardinal; and to all the liberty of living according to their humor, and of displaying and blessing the Host, in company with Sappho. Among all the amorous Prelates, Leo X. had formed a friendship for Cardinal Bibienna; and had lodged him above himself, on the upper floor of the Vatican. There, amid the warm breezes of the Sea of Ostia, and amid the beatings of the wings of doves, the Cardinal made for himself an aerial retreat, to live therein in the voluptuous deshabillé of the life of Athens.

But in the midst of this erotic prelature there was already a witness, lost in the crowd, a stranger, a Monk with the strong head of the race of the North, the serious eye, the broad chest, the robust body, as if nature had fashioned him in advance, to make of him an athlete of Thought.

In his Germanic candor, he had tried the pilgrimage to Rome, to drink the holy effluence of the soul at the source of all holiness. He looks, and cannot believe what he beholds; he listens, and he cannot believe what the hears. Rome is no longer in Rome, it is all entire in him, a poor obscure Monk of the name of Martin. In despair, he draws his cowl over his face, and flees, groaning, from the city of debauchery.

Then, from the summit of the last hill, he turns once more towards the city, swimming in the haze of the sunset, and pointing it out with his finger to I know not what invisible avenger:

—Ninevah shall perish! he says.

On the desert road where he walks alone with his shadow behind him, he feels his chest expand, and into his heroic heart, vast as the world, he feels enter a new idea: the idea of Reform.

Let us bow with respect; an idea is upon this man; an idea the force of the infinite; who will be able to arrest it?

It is no longer Leo X., it is no longer Charles V., it is no longer the Pope, it is no longer the Emperor, these simple wearers of the purple or the crown, who are the masters of the earth; the master of the earth is he, is this passer-by, unknown to himself and to the world, this Monk, half unfrocked, who is walking, with naked feet, in the dust of the road.

Surely the work on which he is mediating at this moment, in the depth of his soul, may well seem that of a madman; for out of this work there has come, until this hour, nothing but fire and blood. Arnold of Brescia attempted it, and had his reward at the stake. John Huss renewed it; the wind bore away his ashes. Jerome of Prague took it up, and he disappeared in a whirlwind of smoke. Savonarola willed also to defy fate, and on the morrow the current of the Arno bowed over all that remained of the martyr.

No matter, Luther has faith. "If thou hast faith, do always that which thou fearest to do," said afterwards a son of his spirit. He goes then intrepidly whither the secret voice of the idea urges him. It comes from afar, this idea; I see it come, from the remoteness of the Middle Age, between a double line of funeral pyres, echelonned along his path, like so many funeral torches; it comes pale, aghast, its two hands upon its forehead, shaking from the folds of its robe the flames of the *autos de fe;* it nevertheless moves onward with a step tragical but firm, until it has found Luther, until it has taken him by the hand, until it has shown him to the world: Behold the man.

Chapter II.

THE SHADOW.

Behold the man, indeed. He speaks, he compares the text of the Messiah with the Commentary of the Church; he finds that one gives the lie to the other, and he makes of the conscience of the faithful, the veritable interpretation of the word of Jesus. From this moment, he denies the mediation of the Clergy between Christ and the Christian, that is to say, the very principle of the Theocracy.

Power blended with everything, Power above everything, Catholicism confiscates Humanity, Religious Power: It receives the infant in the cradle, it marks him with the sign of baptism; it gives him for father the godfather, and for name the name of a saint, to show that there is family above the family; it takes him again afterwards from the arms of the mother to teach him the Catechism, and to lead him to the Eucharist.

Domestic Power: It marries the man; it regulates love; it fixes the time of labor; it ordains the day of rest; it counts the hours for the Faithful; it rises with him, it prays with him at his awakening; it seats itself by the side of him at the table, and dictates to him his meal; here is that thou shalt eat, and this that thou shalt not eat. It fashions the robe of the wife, and shares with him her beauty; it places her head upon the pillow by the side of the husband; in a word it holds all the moments and all the senses of the man as with the hand; it follows him, step by step, from the first to the last minute, and it does not give up the flesh, which it received all warm at its birth, until after it has sealed it up under the stone of the tomb. It did not even relinquish it there: the soul of the dead continued to be its property.

Edifying Power: It makes the life of all serve for the edification of each, and the life of each for the edification of all. It has a voice at the summit of the belfry to cry out upon the air the internal chronicle of the family. When a man is born, the voice speaks; when he marries, it speaks; when he dies, it tolls; when he goes to the scaffold, it rings the punishment. The Priest, in fine, marks with his signature that is to say, with the cross, the limit of the road, the sign of the street, the door of the merchant, the plank of the ship, the ornament of the woman. It scatters the cross everywhere, on the plain, upon the hill, over the city, on the highway. It twenty times puts a gesture in the hand of the passer-by, before the indefinitely repeated image of the crucifix, so that the stone, that the atmosphere, that the dust, that everything says to him: cross thyself and pray.

Teaching Power: The Clergy alone learns, alone speaks, alone writes, alone teaches, and teaches without control, gram-

mar, science, philosophy, history. It puts its hand between the
light and the eye of the understanding, and the world sees only
through it, thinks only in it, and for fear that with age the Faithful may forget the lesson, the Church summons him on Sunday
to the foot of the pulpit, and to the power of the word adds the
pomp of worship, the intoxication of the perfume, the majesty of
architecture, the caress of music. It enters into him through
all the door-ways of the soul; after having effected the convic-
tion of each, it makes also the opinion of each. It has always
on the road an army of preaching brothers, a kind of ambula-
tory telegraph, which goes sowing from frontier to frontier the
general orders of the Papacy.

Heavenly Power: The Priest exercises a kind of superinten-
dence over Nature; the drought is devouring the harvest, he
raises a finger, and makes the rain fall; an epidemic is desola-
ting the population, he orders nine days' devotion, and Death
takes to flight; a man foams at the mouth and howls, is one
possessed, the Exorcist touches him, and the Démon disappears.
The Church has, in fine, a special Saint for every malady, a
specific pilgrimage for each infirmity; some one is dying, it
brings a relic near, and the person at the point of death revives.
It has, in fine, the gift of miracle. It is it which does it, it is it
which asserts it, and to prove that it touches Heaven with its
hands, it is it which canonizes the Elect, and conducts him into
Paradise.

Civil Power: The Clergy holds the book of life, it registers
the certificate of birth, the certificate of decease, the certificate
of marriage; itself it determines the case of obstacle, it proclaims the indissolubility of the household; but it adjudicates the
question of nullity, and gives, in case of need, a dispensation or
divorce. It absorbs the Commune in the Parish, and the Civil
Law in the Canon Law; it excommunicates the loan on interest,
that is to say, the very condition of credit. It enters, in fine,
into every corporation and gives a Saint for manager.

Financial Power: The Pope tariffs vice, he sells innocence;
he levies tribute without limit upon Christianity, under the pretext of dispensation, of year's revenue of Benefices, of reserve of
Benefices, of expectative of Benefices, of St. Peter's penny; but
if the Papacy receives much, it spends more; it incessantly needs
to borrow. The Church forbids the loan upon interest; it creates
sinecure upon sinecure, which it afterwards puts up at auction;
sinecure of Knight of St. Peter, of Notary, of Prothonotary; and
when the name chances to be wanting, of Stradiot and of Mame-
luke; in reality, it furnishes an annuity for a capital invested;
it so makes Rome the exchange of the world, and draws to it
the scum of stock-jobbing; gold flows thereunto in abundance.

Territorial Power: The Clergy everywhere possesses the

third of the land, and upon the land an innumerable army of serfs, laborers, farmers, furnishers, debtors; what is more, by virtue of a text of Moses, it claims over all land a kind of divine right, which constitutes it universal proprietor of the whole world. By virtue of this judaïcal title, it confiscates, it transfers proprietorship, what do I say! power, the Crown; it makes a sign, and Simon of Montfort usurps the county of Toulouse, and the Duke of Anjou chases Manfred from Sicily; the Pope has no need of an army: a word suffices. Innocent III. cries, from the back of his mule, stretching his hands towards the North: Sword, leap from the scabbard, sharpen thyself to slay; and the sword slays of itself. If it does not gain the victory, it sanctifies it by singing a *Te Deum,* and where it does not reign, it sanctifies power; with a drop of oil it fabricates a dynasty.

Judicial Power: It exercises a triple jurisdiction; a primary jurisdiction conjointly with the lay magistracy; it hangs Christ over the tribunal; it publishes the admonition to all who know of crime committed to come forward and made disclosure; it furnishes the formula of the oath; it leads the guilty to the door of the Church; it receives his public confession and petition for pardon; it accompanies to the scaffold him who is to suffer the extreme penalty, for it is necessary that the multitude should see the robe of the Priest in every spectacle which strikes the imagination and gives evidence of power.

A second personal jurisdiction, purely religious, in the tribunal of penitence; there, the Priest binds and releases the soul of the sinner; there, he hears the beating of the heart; there, he wrenches the secret from the conscience, and gives or refuses absolution; but for every sin he has inflicted a moral punishment; fasting, and sometimes flagellation; and the sinner's soul, gone forth from the confessional, eased of the burden of the sin, readily returns to seek a new patent of innocence.

A third jurisdiction, half religious, half laical: The Church invents a metaphysical crime, heresy; an imaginary crime, sorcery; and it institutes the Tribunal of the Inquisition to punish what? an action, a fault? No, a word; less than that, a thought. The Inquisition works in the darkness, behind the grating; accuses upon a mysterious denunciation, it imprisons upon an anonymous testimony, it interrogates in secret, it proceeds underground, it falsifies the truth to deceive the accused, it receives against him every kind of deposition, it refuses to admit for his justification any witness in exculpation, it lends the ear against him to perjury, as if perjury imported verity ,in a process of heresy; it compels under penalty of death, the heretic to be his own denouncer; it invents a new crime, that of not denouncing one's self for chastisement; it tortures to extract from the flesh, crushed by pain, an admission, no matter what, provided it be an admission; it tortures as pleases itself, taking care to protect in advance that death, if death occurs in the middle of the questioning, will be chargeable to the account of the accused; it condemns to an arbitrary punishment, unlimited, to imprisonment, for the time that may suit itself, for a year, ten years, twenty years, forever; and when it releases the prisoner, after his long martyrdom, it imposes silence on him, under the penalty of death at the stake.

But, if the accused refuses to confess a crime which he has neither committed nor understood, there is no pity, it releases him, that is to say, it delivers him to the executioner praying him to spare the blood of the guilty. It is spared, indeed: the victim is burned, and, to crown the raillery, the word pardon is inscribed on the banner which precedes the funeral procession of the *auto da fe;* the Inquisition interrogates, smiling; and kills, lying.

Thus Catholicism intervenes in everything, reigns everywhere; it makes law, opinion, rain, war, medicine, labour, repose. It says to the Soul: Thou belongest to me; to me, to will in thy will, and to think in thy thought; if I abandon thee for a moment, thou fallest into sin or into heresy. I am the Truth, I am Infallibility: believe or die: here is my faith, there a firebrand. Choose!

It has a foot on every hearth, a stare into every conscience, a word on every lip, a voice in every breath, a right in every existence, so that wherever the shadow of the Cross rests, no man can live, think, act, marry, work, be in the agony of death, die, without its permission or out of its presence. It so penetrates all human substance with its own substance, that it is in us a second life, which has expelled from our body the first life which God had given us. You may take afterwards this humanity of new creation, analyze it, re-analyze it, bray it to powder, and you shall not be able to find, in all this mass, re-made, impregnated and kneaded by Catholicism, a fibre, a molecule, a drop of blood, which is not the Church.

Moreover, when excommunication has smitten a city, when the Priest has extinguished prayer, with the flame of the taper, upon the altar, when he has closed the Church and planted the fagot before the door, the Catholic Christian has experienced that kind of supernatural terror which living nature experiences at the coming of an eclipse. Believing Europe breathed only with the breath of the Church, and when this atmosphere was of a sudden withdrawn from its respiration, it fell smitten with asphyxia. Then there was produced, during this syncope of humanity, a profound silence, as if the universal gravitation of the world had suspended its movement. Such was the formidable power of excommunication that it drove the dead from his tomb. When by inadvertence the body of one excommunicated had been admitted into the vault of a Chapel, it came to pass that at the moment when the Priest went up to the altar to celebrate the Mass, the stone of the vault burst open itself and vomited out the corpse.

What power could undertake to strive against the Papacy? What hand could raise itself against it, without being immediately crushed? It had undoubtedly needed a great miracle to bring forth from the manger of Bethlehem the universal monarchy of the Church; but it now required a miracle, at least equally as great, to destroy it; for it had so strongly enchained, by its links of iron, the peoples to its dogmas, that no one, in the broad daylight of the living, would have attempted to escape from the slavery.

Attempted? And how? to flee? to die? To flee, you say? But Catholicism had no frontier; but entire humanity would have aligned itself along the pathway of the fugitive, to cry: Behold the man accursed! and the stone of the road would have leaped up under his feet to stone him. To die? But death did not defraud the Church of its proprietorship of the man. It picked up the body and dragged it on a hurdle to the common sewer.

This is what Papacy was. . . .

And now, when the traveler goes from Florence to Rome, he traverses the fertile valleys of Tuscany, so peopled that the sound the bell has not time to die between two belfries. He sees everywhere a gracious Nature smiling on man, his companion of labour. He advances from culture to culture, under the triumphal arches of vines, as through a perpetual ovation of the country. At every milestone he blesses that policy of philosophical governments which develops itself in harvests.

But, after two days' travel, the long garland of vine branches which accompanied him, from maple tree to maple tree, ends; cultivation disappears, the desert begins. He has before him a plain closed in the south by Mount Albano, and in the north by the Corneto, and he walks over a tumefied soil, much shaken on the day of the Genesis, sometimes bare, and sometimes covered with a sward of the color of bitumen; and he ascends and again descends, incessantly, a rolling line of abrupt hills, scattered on the right and left like lumps of earth on a furrow; from time to time he has a glimpse, in a fold of the land, of a series of white points surmounted by a cupola. It is there.

The fire still broods under the volcanic cinder of the pozzolana; here and there a crevice lets escape a fetid breath, by an invisible vent-hole; or sometimes again the gaping wound of a solfatara contains a stream, level with the surface, bearing sometimes in its current a floating basket of verdure.

Over it is no trace of population or cultivation; neither villa nor village, nor tree, nor vine, nothing but the road, which stretches away as far as one can see, and from time to time an idle breeze which carries away the dust in a whirl, which disappears for an instant, and begins further on a new whirlwind.

And so he goes on, for hours and hours, without perceiving around him the shadow of a living being, unless possibly in the distance, on the crest of some little hillock, the silhouette of a spectre on horseback, with musket on his shoulder. From the immobility of the man and his being mounted, one would term him the petrified sentinel of a dead land, condemned to stand his guard eternally. It is a shepherd who watches a flock hidden in a fold of the ground.

If by chance the traveler leaves the road, to look at some old piece of a wall, forgotten by time, he wakens in the grass a snake, which, scandalized at hearing the footsteps of man, rears up its head, and seems to say: I reign here. It does, indeed, divide the sovereignty of this desert with the lizard and the porcupine.

And always he moves on. And in viewing this resting place of a people inhumed here, grow incessantly of itself, and sink indefinitely under the horizon, he asks if it is a bad dream that he is passing through, or a journey.

Perhaps, however, he may at last encounter a living creature lying in his black frock upon a heap of mud. This hero of the "do nothing" is a buffalo, separated from some herd; at the sound of the step of the traveler he raises above his lair his great idiotic face, and follows him a long time with his gaze, spuming in his beard.

This is the Campagna of Rome: Here and there a farm, a tower, a trunk of a tree burned by a shepherd's fire, and standing upright like a black post in his valley of desolation. Long files of aqueducts ascend on the way towards the Sabine, idly crowned with bouquets of dry grass; the suspended rivers, which once flowed in the air, have flowed back towards their source, arcade by arcade, and now they sleep in their first basin. The mutilated aqueduct still remains standing; a pedestal abandoned by the Naiad.

And still he moves on. The shadow lengthens before him; he quickens his steps as if to escape from the influence of an infernal spell, for, as the day declines, he breathes a thicker air, he feels his steps more heavy, he believes that this sickly earth already holds him by the foot and is about to swallow him; until at last he is able to satisfy himself by a certain sign that man lived there in the XVIth Century. This is a villa, standing on a hill on the right hand, and styled, I believe, the Villa Madama. Raphaël, it is said, decorated it, and if not Raphaël at least his first pupil. Then a pure air breathed there among the vine branches of the trellises, in the alleys of myrtles and of lemon trees. More than one poetic Prelate, like the Cardinal Bembo, undoubtedly fashioned love verses there, with some Muse of the Renascence, under the fine rain and to the sweet complaint of a cascade.

Today, this villa is open to the four winds, and the ravens cross it, from side to side, from one window to the other. Go not thither, when you shall pass by the foot of the hill, above all do not sleep there: you would never wake again, or you would only wake with death in your veins.

And he goes on for some time, and comes in front of a gate opened in an old brick wall, and he reads, upon the broken fragment of the archivault, this Monkish inscription, *Umbra et Nihil,* "shadow and nothing."

The Sun, at this moment, perhaps disappears behind the sloping dome of the pines of the Villa Pamphili, and from the depth of the city arrayed in front of him, in the dazzling vapor of the gloaming, three hundred bells together sound the adieu of Catholicism to the day which is about to die.

Shadow and Nothing, this is then the name of this city; and in effect, apart from two or three quarters more or less modern, more or less alive, you seem to enter into an immense tomb, itself covering two depths of Sepulchres.

First, the Catacombs, those streets delved in the darkness and paved with bones, and then the *Columbaria,* those cisterns full of dust where the old masters of the world sleep, by the side of their slaves, in the old shattered pots.

On the very surface of the soil you will find at every step a tomb; the Cajtel Sant' Angelo, a tomb; the pyramid of Sextus, a tomb; the tower of Capo di Bove, a tomb, and so on; and a wind of death blows from all horizons upon these three stories of death, to sweep from them the last vestiges or rather the last conceits of life.

One can follow the march of the *Malaria,* in some sort, station by station. In the Sixteenth Century, it had halted a league from Rome; in the Seventeenth, it reached the suburbs; in the Eighteenth, it struck at the base of the wall of Circumvallation; in the Nineteenth Century, it penetrated into the city; it already makes a desert of the Vatican, and shuts up, more and more, the scared population in the centre of the city.

You may today lay claim to this widow of two worlds, seated on the bank of its river. The Malaria, from the height of the air, smiles at the claim: it well knows to whom this Queen in mourning will remain.

For the Malaria, dumb as destiny, and terrible as a sentence, strikes with a sure blow, **and defies science and industry** at once. Whence does it come, and how is it to be exorcised? One ought to renounce muttering even an hypothesis, for experience has disconcerted every kind of theory.

The Malaria kills, that is all: an invisible Locusta pours her poison on the wind, one breathes it, and one lives no longer; one remains there prostrate, and waits. It is a slow consumption, a vanishing of force; the heart is extinguished, the blood is coagulated: a spectre, something at once of living and dead: of living, by the envelope, and of dead in the inwardness of the organism; this is the victim of the Malaria.

The river itself of this ruined plain seems to roll in its troubled water I know not what mystery; it runs without making a sound, or rather it is eclipsed under banks of volcanic powder, between the sombre walls of houses draped with rags; on emerging from this land of shadows, it spreads out on coming to the sea, and disappears in a·lagune.

At the extremity of this city of dust, surrounded by precincts of fever, there is a palace, or rather a desert, of brick, peopled with frescoes and statues, and in the rear of this palace a long alley of cypresses, which leads, by a feeble murmur, to the cemetery of the Campagna.

There, amid the phantoms of the Past, an old man holds a book open upon his knee; he has laid a finger upon the leaf, to prevent its turning. From time to time his lip moves, it would be believed that he says something; but he no longer knows what to say: no; and while he looks with dulled eye on the world in motion, without seeing it move, the wind of the age turns under his finger the leaf of the book.

Lightning Source UK Ltd.
Milton Keynes UK
UKOW05f0830120317
296392UK00004B/232/P

9 781935 907244